Heads-Up Dreaming

·······

How Your Dreams Can Predict Your
Future and Change Your Life

D1091527

Heads-Up Dreaming

·······

How Your Dreams Can Predict Your
Future and Change Your Life

CARLYLE SMITH, PH.D.

TURNING
STONE
PRESS

First published in 2014 by
Turning Stone Press, an imprint of
Red Wheel/Weiser, LLC
With offices at:
665 Third Street, Suite 400
San Francisco, CA 94107
www.redwheelweiser.com

ISBN (paperback): 978-1-61852-078-4

Cover design by Jim Warner
Cover image: © Valentina Photos/shutterstock

Printed in the United States of America
IBT
10 9 8 7 6 5 4 3 2 1

To Mary Jane,
Danielle, and Valerie

Contents

Introduction

Predicting the Future

We are a species that is continually concerned about the future. We do not even think much about our immediate future as it is such an automatic part of our lives. Our eyes tell us we will soon be walking into a closed door if we do not take appropriate action. We then prepare to open the door or stop walking. We have ears that tell us that the loud sound on our left means that a car is coming and we should stop walking until it has passed. Our senses are busy during every waking moment predicting the immediate future and making sure that we don't come to physical harm.

But we are also concerned with the more distant future. We make conscious plans for routine events each day and prepare for them. What will we eat and what will we wear? Even in a modern world this often means considerable planning and organization; there are many future events that require this kind of preparation and these include such things as job interviews, exams, business meetings, and so on. Of course, despite conscious preparation for these future events, there is still a margin of unpredictability. Those who prepare more thoroughly are more likely to have considered the unexpected, but life is rarely so simple and in many situations, making decisions about the future is based on limited information. There are uncertainties and unknowns that can be almost impossible to overcome when making important choices. Some of the most important decisions that we make include choosing a life partner, buying houses or cars, and dealing with family members. Should you really marry this person that you have only known for less than 1 year? Should you really go into serious debt to buy a house, not knowing if interest rates will rise or if your job will last? These decisions are sometimes made with partial information under considerable stress and, all too often, they are made emotionally rather than logically; this can lead to disastrous long term outcomes. The well meaning advice of parents, friends, and relatives can be helpful, but, in the end, possibly contradictory, somewhat in error, and crippling, as we must learn to make our own decisions.

A Natural Capacity

This book is about the possibility that each of us has the biological capability to reduce the uncertainty in our lives. I "discovered" this capability in myself many years ago and it has been an important factor guiding me to make the best choices possible. I have shared this knowledge with my family, friends, and colleagues and they have all benefitted from it. In fact, most of them are now better at it than I am. The method involves looking at your nightly dreams. Some of these dreams clearly describe future waking events for the dreamer and I have named them "Heads-Up" dreams. Many dream scholars have noted this phenomenon before and I am certainly not the first to talk about it. These dreams could also be described as precognitive dreams, but I have renamed them because the term "precognitive" suggests that the dreams will mostly be about disasters like tsunamis or terrorist attacks. My Heads-Up dreams are much more mundane and largely concern my own health and well-being. I have discovered that my family, friends, colleagues, and students can also experience these kinds of dreams and the first part of the book is a detailed examination of what these dreams look like compared to "normal" or non-Heads-Up dreams.

In later chapters, I describe something even more remarkable. It seems clear that we can also dream about the futures and personal details of others. While I have had this experience a few times, there is a small number of people who are especially gifted in this area. I have included the dreams of one of these individuals. Her specialty is diagnosing health problems in patients unfortunate enough to have been told by doctors that they are not sure what the problem is or worse—that there is no treatment.

Do You Really Want to Know?

Some individuals can't imagine why anyone would want to know their own future. They expect that it will be full of negative prognostications. They would prefer to be "blind-sided" by life's surprises. However, I have found that these dreams do not exclusively provide "written-in-stone" negative scenarios that would scare the dreamer half to death and raise his or her stress levels to dangerous heights. In fact, negative predictions tend to arrive in a timely manner such that the dreamer has an opportunity to change his or her behaviour and reduce or even completely avoid the dream depiction. Furthermore, many of these dreams consist of neutral or positive scenarios. If you like the idea of having as much information as possible to make conscious decisions, you will be interested in knowing more about these dreams—when they occur, how to recognize them, and how to make use of them.

Is There a Scientific Explanation?

I am not sure where these special dreams come from, but it is clear that they are about tomorrow and if acted upon, they do help. My long training and career as a scientist resulted in my forming certain habits concerning the collection and organization of my dreams and the dreams of others. I felt an obligation to categorize them, count them, make some graphs and do some statistics. Although I have been told that I am taking the fun and magic out of dreams portraying the future, I feel that it leads to a better understanding of what makes them unique and recognizable. I also feel that there should be some kind of theory that makes the idea of premonition type dreams more palatable. Often, facts alone are not enough and many people are more reassured about a phenomenon when there is a theory to explain it. To that end, I have proposed a tentative theory that I hope can be revised and improved over time. More importantly, I have provided a list of things that I (and my fellow dreamers) do to maximize the recognition and use of these special kinds of dreams.

Because so many people feel they have actually experienced something like this at least once in their lives, I strongly suspect that we are biologically equipped to do this and all that is needed is some practice. It is my hope that everyone learns to recognize Heads-Up dreams, which can help to guide them, especially through the difficult times in life.

☞ 1 ☜

My Initial Interest in Dreams

My interest in dreams began when I was a graduate student in Psychology at the University of Waterloo, in Waterloo, Canada. It was the late 1960s and the climate for exploring the mind, pharmacologically at least, was in high gear all over North America. It had been reported in *Science* some years earlier that sleep had a number of different states with very different physiology and that one state, Rapid Eye Movement (REM) sleep was a separate state where dreaming took place. This sleep state repeated itself four or five times a night. I was fascinated with these reports and began to read everything I could about sleep and dreams. It did not take long for me to realize that dreams had been of interest to humanity for many years before I was even born. However, as a budding neuroscientist, my interest was even greater than average curiosity because of the facts associated with the discovery of the REM sleep state and the special physiology of those time periods. I decided I would keep a written account of my own dream experiences and a log of my day activities, as well. My secret hope was that I would find some kind of wisdom in my dreams that was unique and maybe even superior to the thoughts of my waking mind. Furthermore, I thought I might actually discover something about dreams that no one else had ever considered.

I had come from a family that was not necessarily interested in dreams and I could only remember one from my entire childhood and teenage years. When I decided to collect dreams, I found the process difficult and time consuming. My dreams were relatively short and if I did not have absolute quiet when I woke up, the memory of the dream would disappear. I was awed by the fact that my girlfriend could remember two or three dreams per night and they were often hundreds of words in length when she wrote them down. The point is, it has always been a constant struggle for me to remember my dreams and no one would ever consider me to be a "gifted" dreamer with special abilities of any kind.

As I began to delve into the available literature, I found that books on dreams were quite diverse and while there were a lot of opinions, the idea that one could get meaning from his or her own dreams was not nearly as easy as I had hoped. I became convinced that the Freudian approach was not for me, despite the fact that Freudian theory and ideas were prominent in many of my psychology courses. I found the writings of Jung fascinating, but the examples of his dreams and the dreams of his patients seemed way more complex and interesting than anything I had ever experienced. My dreams seemed to be very mundane by comparison and I even worried that I might not be a normal dreamer. I purchased several "dream dictionaries" which claimed to translate the symbols that I could not understand—but I found these dictionaries often did not agree on any particular symbol. Further, when I did decide on a listed symbolic meaning,

I had trouble relating it to my current life situation. Looking through my little collection of dreams at this point in my life, I had to admit that I did not really see anything of value in them at all. Then I had a dream that I found quite curious.

> **Dream, February 20, 1970.** *I am in my office and it is slightly different. MJ is there and GS comes in to see it. He is amazed at how nicely it is fixed up. I tell him jokingly that I don't think that I will have the stereo put in as there is so little time left for me to stay.*

Later that same day, GS, a fellow graduate student, did come to my office—the first time he actually had dropped by in about a month. MJ (my girlfriend) was there, as well. She had dropped in to see me briefly. GS admired my office, especially the new cover on my chair and the new painting a friend had given me to brighten the place up. I joked that I was not going to bother putting in a stereo system as I wouldn't be in the room for that long. Our mindset was that we would soon graduate and get jobs, so talk soon turned to devising strategies for getting employment. At one point the conversation was about some possible drug company positions available for newly graduated PhDs that GS had heard about. While we were talking, I realized that I had dreamed that something like this had already happened, just last night. The offices that we had when I was a PhD student were neither large nor luxurious. We were housed in an old factory that had been renovated to accommodate us and we decorated the drab rooms ourselves to brighten them up. Since I was near to graduating, I did not considered it to be of major importance to spend a lot of time decorating.

Besides, few people visited these rooms that served as both offices and labs. It was an unusual event for GS to actually come in and look inside my little office and quite a coincidence that my girlfriend was there, too.

The feeling that I had dreamed this scenario, although not perfectly, led me to search for descriptions of similar experiences. One concept, "déjà vu" or "already seen" appeared to describe what I had experienced and the term had been coined by a French researcher, Emile Boirac, in the 1800s. The individual typically reports that they had already witnessed the real-life event they were now experiencing and very often the original experience was a dream. More recently, this concept has been divided into more precise categories, but the prevailing idea that the waking "déjà vu" experience may have been preceded by a dream still persists and a more appropriate description has been suggested—"déjà rêvé" or "already dreamed."

Over the years I have discovered that many people have had such an experience at least once or twice in their lives, but because it has happened so rarely, it is easy to dismiss or ignore and often it does not portray any really important life events, just little insignificant episodes. As I continued to collect dreams over the years, I discovered that a certain number of them fell into this "preview" category. They appeared to be dreams about something that happened later the same day. This was a situation that defied the concept of time. I did excitedly tell some of my fellow graduate students, but the response at that time was either less than enthusiastic or aroused the suspicion that I had been smoking more than cigarettes (I was, at that time, smoking 60–65 cigarettes per day). I became wary of mentioning that I was having these kinds of dreams to those around me not sympathetic to such ideas, for fear of losing all credibility. However, I did continue to collect and record my dreams. As the years went by I came up with my own kinds of expectations about my dreams and the dreams of those close to me, including family and friends. It was a very practical kind of expectation that my dreams would sometimes provide me with information that would help me to make the best choices in life, from the very important to the very trivial. Because a small proportion of my dreams seemed to be the kind that were capable of coming up with this information *before* the real-life event occurred, I began to watch all of my dreams with this idea in mind. At first the dreams seemed to only provide very trivial information, and I would realize that my dream had apparently predicted some later event, but what took place certainly did not change my life. As time went on, I noticed that the information changed and was sometimes quite important and had I known that this or that particular dream was about an important future life event, the "heads-up" information would have been very valuable.

As a professor of psychology, I have given a course on dreams and dreaming for almost twenty years. A question that I ask the class is: *Is it possible to dream about the future?* Very few, if any, hands go up to answer the question. However, when I ask how many have had the experience of dreaming about someone they have not seen in a long while and subsequently meet that person or have some sort of contact with them, approximately 50% of the class raise their hands. I then point out that they already knew the answer to my first question and it is "*Yes*"—at least sometimes.

In the following chapters, I will describe what these Heads-Up dreams look like, both my own and those of family, friends, and colleagues who have provided me with accounts of theirs.

Blind Spots

While I continued to write down my dreams and keep a day diary, I also began to ask about the dreams of those around me. I began to notice something that clinicians or anyone examining the dreams of someone else have known for a long time. It is often easier for an "outsider" to guess the meaning of a dream than it is for the person who had the dream. The dreamer is actually very likely to conclude that their dream experience made no sense and was not related to their own life situation. For example, one night at a party, a woman, who had heard about my interest in dreams, approached me. She told me her "silly" dream and confided to me that it made no sense. She was confident that she was not telling me anything very important about herself, certainly nothing embarrassing. She did not mind that several other people were listening. (It helps to know that this woman had a sharp tongue and her relatives and friends were all wary of her.)

> **Dream of Woman:** I am in the center of a circle of friends. But they are all facing away from me and I feel they don't want much to do with me. I notice that my tongue is a Gillette blue (razor) blade.

The meaning of the dream seemed so obvious that many listeners realized what the woman was trying to tell herself and there were some sly smiles of recognition. With her "sharp" tongue, the woman was turning her friends away because of her caustic comments. Anyone could have told her this anyway, but probably would not dare, as "the tongue" might turn on them. Amazingly, *she* did not get it! She seemed not to notice what many around her had immediately understood. For some reason, often, the dreamer is the last to know. This dream demonstrated how important it can be to have someone else hear the dream, or even to have the dreamer hear the dream read to them by someone else. It does not have to be a dream expert. This "blind spot" is so powerful that it allows someone to imagine that the dream they had is useless fluff when, in fact, it makes a great deal of sense to friends and acquaintances. Trying to relate dream activity to waking daily life can be difficult if one works alone and it is undoubtedly one of the reasons that many individuals quickly conclude that their dreams are nonsensical and unimportant.

Interestingly, telling the individual what the dream "means" or what you think it means for them, does not always solve the "blind spot" problem. Even if you are somehow essentially correct, the effect on the dreamer may not be the best. For example, in the case of the woman at the party, one could simply announce to the dreamer that she should try to curb her nasty tongue and be nicer to everyone. However, that might (and did, although I tried to be very diplomatic) simply get a response of denial. This dreamer explained to me that she was typically frank and honest with her friends, but certainly not mean and nasty, and that the dream analyzer (me) was being unfair and overly critical. The dreamer has to have that moment of insight that allows them to realize that this material is theirs and that their brain has somehow created it. Insights often take time and it is only after the insights that individuals begin to think about changing their behavior.

In my student years, there were no dream groups or dream experts around with which to share dreams. This made deciphering my own dreams often difficult or fruitless. However, the woman with the nasty tongue had apparently, at some level, been able to tell herself, in the dream state, that she was in danger of losing her friends if she continued to be so blunt. So, I persisted in believing that some dreams might convey important, even vital information to me, if I could just figure out the symbolism. Of course I was certainly not the first person to come to such a conclusion, but, at the time, I felt as if I was onto some kind of amazing discovery. When looking at the dreams of others, I have discovered that the personal "blind spot" seems just as active for Heads-Up dreams as for any other kind of dreams. My wife and children often told me their dreams in the morning (which I carefully wrote down) and then later, when they described their day, I was able to point out that their dream had somewhat predicted their adventures. At first they were not completely sure, but then, after some reflection, realized that they had indeed had a Heads-Up dream about a small segment of a notable waking experience that day. The realization came slowly, but the reaction was almost always one of surprise. With time, they all became adept at spotting Heads-Up dreams and at using the information to their advantage.

⁓ 2 ⁓

The "Heads-Up" Dream

In the early days of looking at my own dreams, my routine was to write them down first thing in the morning, date them, and then look back at them from time to time, perhaps once every week or every ten days. I was able spot the particular predictive quality in my dreams, mostly because I had the dream written down and could be sure of the exact dream content. While I virtually never had the dream in front of me when the corresponding waking event took place, I was now aware of the possibility of a dream/waking connection and was able to look up the dream. I wrote and dated comments under the dream when something about it seemed to be connected with a waking life event. As time went on, I became more confident that my dreams might be a preview of a later waking event and would keep them in the back of my mind as the day progressed. I began to think of them as Heads-Up dreams as they alerted me to a possible similar event in my subsequent waking life.

Dream, August 16, 1979: Seems that in looking in an old purse, I find a folded 500 franc note as well as some Canadian money.

Comment later that day: *When MJ got out her little plastic folder, from her purse, to give me a blank check so that I could fill it out, there was a folded 500 Franc note, which fell out. Both of us had forgotten about this money. There was also some Canadian money that MJ knew about (although I did not).*

This dream was a very typical Heads-Up dream which I had while we were living in Nice, France. I was spending some time at the University of Nice to possibly obtain an automatic sleep recording system that was being developed there. Nice is a fantastic place if you are rich, but if your cash flow is limited, then a bit more care is required to manage resources. We lived with our two year-old daughter in the bottom half of a very nice villa, but the rent was just manageable and there were a lot of other expenses, so we had to count our pennies. MJ kept the checks for our French bank in her purse in a plastic folder. I never touched her purse, but I counted on her to have the checks on hand when we needed them. While shopping that afternoon, we decided to pay for the items by check. To the surprise of both of us, there was an unexpected and very pleasant bonus. Folded in behind the cheques was a 500F note which was worth about $200 Canadian at the time. We were delighted at this find. There was also some Canadian money, which MJ knew was tucked inside, but I did not. I considered my dream about this to be a Heads-Up dream for several reasons. The finding of the extra 500F note was a pleasant surprise to both of us. It was not found in an old purse, but it was found in MJ's daily purse as opposed to my wallet or in a drawer. I was unaware of the Canadian money that she had as well.

This is typical of the kind of dream I have had from time to time throughout my adult life. I had written it down earlier, was able to check the corresponding details between dream events and real-life events. If I had only observed one or two of these types of dreams, I would, of course, have considered them to be coincidental. However, after forty years and several hundred carefully documented dream cases, I don't think that "coincidence" is an adequate explanation.

For many years, I tried to record as many dreams as I could from my wife in order to expand my Heads-Up dream database. MJ was (and still is) a prolific dreamer. While my dreams averaged about 60–90 words (written out, after waking), hers often ran into the hundreds of words range. While I was happy to remember a single dream for the night, she could remember two or three. It soon became clear that her ability to have Heads-Up dreams was superior to mine. Here is an example of one of MJ's first Heads-Up dreams, before we were married, that amazed us both. In order to fully understand this dream, it should be understood that I was, at this time, a graduate student, enrolled in the Biopsychology graduate program at the University of Waterloo, taking courses in both biology and psychology. (Such a program would likely now be considered a Neuroscience program.) The offices/labs were so arranged that each graduate student had his or her desk and bookshelves in the same room as the apparatus for the experimental project. The projects could involve studying rats, mice, lizards, or goldfish (to name some of the species). My project involved studying sleep in rats and my office/lab housed my desk and books as well as cages for my rats and an EEG machine to record their brainwave activity while they slept. One morning, MJ told me the following dream that I faithfully wrote down.

> **Dream of MJ, January 1970:** *I was sitting in Carlyle's lab when two of my friends, Sue and John, came in to talk to me and Carlyle. Carlyle went out to get something up near GJ's room and while he was away, the rats got loose. They were crawling on the black floor and I was catching them and putting them back in their boxes. Then I saw rat #34 bleeding down beside the tub. I called for Carlyle then ran to get him. He came carrying some stuff and was not upset at all. Then I remember someone cooking some kind of good smelling custard. He had on a white lab coat and really wasn't in his lab, but we could see him. B and H and some girls were in B's office and decided to go for Chinese food. They tried to convince Carlyle to go. He said "No, but bring some back for us." Then we seemed to be in a convertible driving with the top down. We went to a Chinese restaurant.*

At first glance, it might seem that this was a very confused dream, possibly without much meaning. The dream was interesting in that several waking life events happened later that day that had eerie correspondence to the dream content. While there may have been some important overall deeper symbolic message or meaning for MJ, it has never become apparent to either of us. On the other hand, it definitely previewed a large number of unusual real-life events later the same day.

In order to evaluate these dreams, I tried to come up with a method that could classify the dream elements and relate them to the subsequent waking life events that were experienced. Trying to assess the actual probabilities of dreaming about a future event has proved daunting. However, an easier way to compare those parts of the dream that correspond to waking events is to provide a numerical score for each dream/waking similarity or "hit" (See Table 1).

Table 1. MJ's Heads-Up dream fragments and corresponding waking events.

	Dream Event Fragment	Corresponding Waking Event
1)	I was sitting in Carlyle's lab... Carlyle went out to get something.	MJ is in my rat sleep lab, alone. I have stepped out to get something for my experiment.
2)	...the rats got loose. They were crawling on the black floor.	Rats escape out onto the floor (painted black) of the lab while I am gone and MJ is there alone.
3)	...I was catching them and putting them back in their boxes.	MJ scoops them up and puts them back in their cages.
4)	...I saw rat #34 bleeding down beside the tub.	Rat # 34 had a dark red stain on his tummy and it looked bad.
5)	...I called for Carlyle then ran to get him. He came carrying some stuff and was not upset at all.	I realize #34 had only gotten some red EEG recording ink on his white tummy. It just looked like he was bleeding. He was fine.
6)	Then I remember someone cooking some kind of good smelling custard.	E was cooking a meagre evening meal as he worked—custard pudding of some sort.

(Continued)

7)	*He had on a white lab coat and really wasn't in his lab, but we could see him.*	E paced up and down the hall in his white lab coat.
8)	*B and H and two girls were in B's office and decided to go for Chinese food. They tried to convince Carlyle to go.*	B and H come by with two girls. They invite us to join them at the nearby Chinese restaurant for dinner.
9)	*He said "No, but bring some back for us."*	I decline as I have to finish my EEG recording session.
10)	*Then we seem to be in a convertible driving with the top down.*	We can't get my car to go and so wind up borrowing E's convertible.
11)	*We go to a Chinese restaurant.*	We go to the regular Chinese restaurant.

1) I scored the fact that MJ was alone in my lab. When I was sleep recording, I needed to be there all of the time. However, I really needed to get some equipment and so I asked MJ to keep an eye on things and stepped out and down the hall to another room. The errand only took a few minutes, but in that time, things went very wrong while MJ was left alone. *Dream/Waking Score =1.*

2) Because I was planning to be away from the lab for only a few minutes, I did leave the animals such that they had the potential to get out of their cages, but thought I would be back immediately. This was the only time in two years that several rats actually jumped out onto the black painted floor. *Score = 1.*

3) MJ was not squeamish and began to pick up the escaped rats and put them back in their cages. *Score =1*

4) The fact the MJ dreamed of rat # 34 as being the one that would knock over a red polygraph ink bottle-dispenser and get some on himself was remarkable. There were 6 rats that could have escaped. Three did go for a little walk around the room before MJ picked them up (they were very tame). Only # 34 got into mischief and managed to knock over a small bottle of ink and get a red ink stain on his white fur. *Score = 2*

5) When MJ called out the door for me to come and see, I was already coming back down the hall. I entered the room and at first glance, #34 *did* look bad. But I quickly realized that it was red ink rather than blood and so was not too upset. *Score =1*

6) My colleague, another PhD student, E, usually brought a supper or went out to eat. But that day, because of his schedule and because of the cold, stormy weather, he decided to cook something in the lab. That "something" was a custard pudding of some kind and the smell wafted down the hall. *Score =1*

7) While MJ did not actually see E in her dream, she did see *someone* (a male) in a white lab coat, pacing up and down the hall. Since we all wore white lab coats, and E sometimes was in the hall, this part of the dream did not seem so amazing. However, on this day, E was indeed pacing up and down the hall in his lab coat, not just because of his cooking but because of his experiment. He did not want to distract his bar-pressing rats. *Score =1*

8) Several hits occur here. B and H had labs nearby (B's was right across the hall) and I saw them every day.

However, neither was married nor had a girlfriend at that time. The fact that they *both* came by *with* female companions to invite us to go to the restaurant was quite unusual. The invitation was spontaneous as well, and they invited us on their way out, when they saw both of us at the door to my lab. *Score = 2*

9) The invitation would normally have been gladly accepted. However, I was simply not able to go until my rats had finished their nap. So, I declined for MJ and myself. *Score =1*

10) Later that night, when I was finally finished sleep recording, we realized that we were quite hungry. We decided after considering several restaurant possibilities, that we would go to the Chinese restaurant, even though our chances of connecting with B and H and their friends was slim. We shouted "goodbye" to E and stepped out into the snow. As it turned out, the temperature was quite low (-25° F). On top of this, it had been snowing and the wind was now blowing snow around. We got into my car (which was definitely not new) and one turn of the key told me what winter drivers all eventually experience—a click—the sound of a dead battery that will not turn over the motor. Disappointed, we went back into the building. There was E, still hard at work, and he greeted us with a "That was fast!" When we explained our problem, he reached into his pocket and handed me the keys to his car—a convertible sports car. This was a very nice gesture and we thanked him. It is the only time I ever drove (or rode in) E's car, although I worked down the hall from him for over two years. *Score =1*

11) We did debate over several restaurants and because of the time, we knew that trying to get to the Chinese restaurant before it closed would be tight. However, we decided to go for it, as we both were in the mood for Chinese food. *Score = 1*

Not every single facet of the dream came true. Sue and John did not come by in the dream, although they sometimes did. We did not drive E's car with the top down as it was the dead of winter and the temperature was -25° F. Despite these "inaccuracies," it would be difficult to convince us that this dream did not give us a heads-up about our unusual day. The total "hit" score here was thirteen. By comparison to my dreams, this is a very high score. In the chapters ahead, I will dissect the dreams in the same way as this one. However, since the numerical scores for "hits" are fairly obvious, I will not include them with the dreams described in future chapters. I have scored all of the dreams that I have collected to track my progress over the years and to compare my dreams with the dreams of others. I must say that almost everyone who has given me dreams is at least as talented as I am and I have come to the conclusion that if I can do it, virtually everyone can.

$\backsim 3 \backsim$

More Heads-Up Dreams

For graduate students in the late 60s–early 70s, the system for getting information about the publications of other scientists was far more laborious than it is today, where most papers can immediately be downloaded as PDFs. Publication reprints of interest were gleaned from booklets that simply listed all of the articles in neuroscience type journals, with no added information except the title of the publication and the name and address of the author. Even worse for students, these booklets cost a considerable amount and were out of range of modest budgets. They became available from one's supervisor of studies only after he or she had finished with it. The process required filling out, by hand, and sending a small request card in the mail to the author. These request cards were typically made out in little piles of 10–20 at a time and then tossed in the mail. They would eventually find their way to the author at his or her institution and then, if the author had any reprints left, he or she would send you one. If none were left, you would only rarely receive a "sorry" note saying that there were no more papers left. Since scientific journals used to provide 50–100 complementary copies of the published paper free to the author to give out as he or she wished, sometimes there were no papers left to give out. Add in that some authors were from universities in other countries combined with the uncertainties of the "snail mail" system, and you have a very low probability of predicting if and when a particular paper would arrive, if ever. I describe this "60s state of the art" mail system because it helps to show how the following dream information could not have been discovered by alternate means.

> **Dream, March 23, 1970.** *I see the word "Chlor..." and maybe ending with "...in" or "...id." Apparently it is the name of a very important drug which could have some value for sleep, perhaps not preventing REM (dreaming) sleep. Underneath the drug was written a very scientific description that I cannot remember (Table 2).*

Table 2. Dream, March 23, 1970.

	Dream Event Fragment	Corresponding Waking Event
1)	*I see the word "Chlor..." and maybe ending with "...in" or "...id."*	The article in the mail is about Chloral Hydrate vs. Glutethimide and Methylprylon.
2)	*Apparently it is the name of a very important drug which could have some value for sleep, perhaps not preventing REM (dreaming) sleep.*	Chloral hydrate is found to be the only drug that does not disturb REM sleep, impair dream recall, or disturb mood.
3)	*Underneath the drug was written a very scientific description that I cannot remember.*	The paper has a long discussion of the experimental procedure, results, and discussion.

1) That same day, right after writing down my dream from the night before, I looked in my mailbox and found one piece of mail. It was a reprint entitled, "Effects of Hypnotics on Sleep Patterns, Dreaming and Mood State: Laboratory and Home Studies" by A. Kales et al., 1969. The paper talks about the effects on sleep and dream recall in participants following administration of one of the drugs. While I did not actually recall the exact names (who knows if I actually did dream the exact full names and did not remember them?), but there were tantalizing similarities with these complicated drug names in my dream.

2) The drug that stood out in the study (chloral hydrate) seemed to be the drug that I dreamed would not interfere with REM sleep. Drugs for insomnia were at that time notorious for selectively reducing REM sleep and this left the patient feeling tired since it was not normal sleep. The more sophisticated drugs of today do a better job, but at that time, chloral hydrate was judged to be the best for avoiding the problem.

3) The paper had a long discussion about the methods used and the conclusions reached, although I simply could not remember them. The dream did indicate that I had read something, as opposed to seeing it on TV, or hearing it at a talk, or from another student or professor.

This is typical of my literal Heads-Up dreams with the occurrence of the real-life event being later the same day and with dream events and real-life corresponding events being very similar. As it happened, I had just written this dream down that morning about an hour before

I checked my mail. Also typical of this experience, after reading this scientific paper, it slowly dawned on me that this was a very peculiar happening and checked my written dream for that day. There was no premonition beforehand or any special feeling about this event and if I had not written down the dream I could have easily missed the phenomenon entirely. But there was no doubt about the timing. I had written the dream and then, shortly after, found the paper in the mail.

Here is another Heads-Up dream, which has more symbolic events and, in spots, is not as literally accurate, but it was a once in a life-time event and seemed to qualify:

> **Dream, June 4, 1971.** *I am pulling two fish out of a sort of tank at home. I believe they are white fish or are certainly white coloured. Everyone at home seems to be watching for me to finish with the fish…My parents have already eaten and they are waiting for me to eat. Then the scene becomes one of me going along a fence line with some people and then coming back again. The fence posts have markings on them that seem to be psychology symbols. I exit out the door of a university (Table 3).*

Table 3. Dream, June 4, 1971.

	Dream Event Fragment	Corresponding Waking Event
1)	*Pulling fish out of a sort of tank.*	Pulling fish out of a pool, formed by a waterfall and sharp turn in the river.

(Continued)

2)	*Pulling two fish out.*	I caught two fish. No one else caught anything worth keeping.
3)	*...they are white fish or are certainly white coloured.*	They were silver bass, which I thought looked like white fish at first.
4)	*My parents have already eaten and they are waiting for me to eat.*	Everyone has eaten but me, and MJ's parents would like me to hurry and eat.
5)	*...going along a fence line with some people and then coming back again.*	...we had to crawl through and walk along a farmer's fence line to get to the fishing spot. We came back the same way.
6)	*The fence posts have markings on them...*	MJ's father is travelling near to where he grew up. He quizzes us several times to see if we know what concession we are on.

While this dream might have some interesting personal meaning for me concerning my career as a psychologist, there were a number of interesting real-life "hits" that occurred later that day that allowed me to score it as a Heads-Up dream, even though the sequence of events was not in the exact order in which I had written down my dream events. Notice that I have followed the real-life sequence below, as it makes more waking sense, even though the dream did not find ordering the events to be as important.

4) I was at my girlfriend's house for the weekend, visiting. I slept in and was woken up by MJ. Everyone had eaten

but me, and MJ's parents (not mine) wanted me to hurry and eat as her father had a surprise for us—a fishing trip to the river that he used to fish as a boy. While I managed to dream the wrong set of parents, the rest of the scenario was correct. It was not typical of me to be the last one up.

5) While we frequently went fishing (MJ, her father, and myself), we always went out on Lake Simcoe in a boat to fish. This particular outing was a surprise to me. We had not planned it and we had to drive for at least an hour to get to this place. Then, we had to leave the truck, crawl through a fence, and walk along a farmer's fence line to get to the fishing spot. It turned out that this is where my girlfriend's father had fished as a boy. We also had to come back to the truck this same way. None of us ever went back to this spot after that day, so it was a "one-time" event in my life.

1) We reached a beautiful little pool area at the bottom of a small waterfall. This spot marked a sharp turn in the river as well. My future father-in-law had chosen the spot not just because it had always been a good fishing spot, but because it was indeed a very pretty place. We all had nibbles at our lines and caught several small fish that, because of their size, we immediately threw back. While we were not pulling fish out of any tank, as I had dreamed, we were getting fish from a confined small pool, so it seemed symbolically right. We were pulling fish out of something like a tank, only one that nature had made.

2) While fishing, I managed to catch two fish, which were considered large enough to keep. MJ caught a tiny rock bass and MJ's father caught a small black bass, but

they were both small and were immediately thrown back. Interestingly, I was the only one to keep my catch. Because I not only dreamed that I would be catching fish that day, I also got the right number of fish.

3) The fish I caught and kept looked like white fish to me. It turned out that they were an unusual strain (called silver bass locally) and only found in that river. They were not seen in the larger lakes nearby. Because I managed to dream focus on the unusual strain of these fish, as well as guess the colour, I considered this to be another hit.

6) While the fence posts did not actually have markings on them as in the dream, on the drive home, my future father-in-law was in fine form and he kept quizzing us to see if we knew which concession line we were on and whether or not we were lost. So, there was an oblique dream reference to numbers on the fence posts.

∽

There were, as usual, some elements in the dream that did not appear that day. Certainly there were no psychology symbols on the fence posts in this rural area and we were nowhere near any university. Furthermore, my parents lived over a thousand miles away and were not waiting for me to wake up. There were, however, a number of remarkable dream/waking correlations and this turned out to be a once in a lifetime event. We never returned to this spot again.

Thus, Heads-Up dreams (mine at least) can contain some elements that appear to faithfully mirror the later real-life events. However, there are also some elements that are symbolic in nature and require a judgement as to whether they constitute an accurate enough prediction of the later real-life event. While I have no precise rule about how many literal elements a dream must have before I can consider it a Heads-Up dream, almost all of them have at least two elements that can be directly related to real-life events. If there are also symbolic elements, it is usually fairly easy to see the symbol/real-life connection. Thus all Heads-Up dreams must have some literal elements that correspond to real-life events.

Along with the scoring of these dreams to assess them as Heads-Up dreams, there is another factor that should be mentioned. This factor is a feeling of recognition that occurs when the dreamer recognizes the close links between the dream and subsequent real-life event. It is similar to the "aha" experience that occurs on suddenly understanding the solution to a problem. For me at least, it is not highly exciting, but there is a very definite realization that the waking events unfolding are ones that were part of an earlier dream. The "déjà vu" phenomenon, mentioned earlier, has often been used to describe this experience. The concept is almost a household word and there was even a movie by that name starring Denzel Washington. One survey revealed that many people reporting these experiences believe that they had previously dreamed the subsequent waking events and a more accurate term, as previously mentioned, might be "déjà rêvé."

I have scored over fifty dreams as being Heads-Ups dreams with the common characteristic that they all happened on the same day as the corresponding real-life event. What I have found is that I could not say that my day would have gone differently had I not discovered these dream/waking connections. In fact, because of the novelty of these dreams, it was only after the waking event that I thought of them at all. There may be some further hidden or beneficial meaning that one could glean from these reports, but I did not discover any. For me, most of these Heads-Up dreams could be classified as "trivial." They were interesting and fun, but had I been aware, when writing them down, that they would be describing what would happen later the same day, I would not have changed my behaviour.

❦ 4 ❦

"Same Day" Heads-Up Dreams That Were Not So Trivial

Some of the Heads-Up dreams turned out to be quite important to my life. If I had known enough to trust what I had seen in the following dream, I might have considered trying to change the outcome—if such a thing is possible. While the following dream was not really disastrous in terms of waking corresponding events, it was not so trivial either, especially for my wife, MJ.

Dream, April 28, 1972. We seem to be driving on the road somewhere and MJ has to get out of the car. Workmen nearby force me to keep driving by waving me on and soon I realize I have left MJ behind. When I try to go back for her, they will not allow me to do so (Table 4).

Table 4. Dream, April 28, 1972.

	Dream Event Fragment	Corresponding Waking Event
1)	*We seem to be driving on the road somewhere and MJ has to get out of the car.*	We decide to drive by the Lyon airport. I stop in front of some main doors and MJ hops out.

(Continued)

2)	*Workmen nearby force me to keep driving by waving me on.*	There are many police around today and they force me to drive on.
3)	*I realize I have left MJ behind.*	As I am forced to continue, I realize I have left MJ behind.
4)	*When I try to go back for her, they will not allow me to do so.*	I try to duck in to a spot farther down and quickly run back for her, but the police immediately spot me and force me to move.

This dream took place while I was doing post-doctoral work in a sleep research laboratory in Lyon, France. We were living in a completely French milieu and while we were coping with the second language, we sometimes yearned to read English. Once in a while, we would pick up an English language newspaper to read. There were few places in Lyon where such a thing could be had and the airport was one of those places. Normally we got the paper at a newsstand downtown, but on this morning we decided we might be able to get the paper at the airport and save some time and traffic congestion.

1) We normally bought the paper downtown, but this morning, spur of the moment, we decided to go and get a paper for MJ at the airport and then drop her back at our apartment as she would be home for the day while I was at the lab. The plan was for her to grab a paper from the newsstand inside and then get back to the car quickly. We drove to the front main departure doors and MJ got out of the car.

2) However, on this day, the main road in front of the airport was lined with police in their blue uniforms. They were not allowing anyone to loiter in front of the main doors. I was waved on immediately and had only enough time to let MJ out. Despite the fact that there were no workmen that would not let me park, the message was clear. (There were always a lot of workmen around Lyon and they became a familiar sight. They worked on all kinds of construction and could be seen anywhere a building project or road repair was going on. They were almost always dressed in dark blue coveralls, the same general colour as the French police uniform.)

3) I realized I left MJ behind and was unable to stay behind, or even drive slowly in order for her to catch up.

4) I continued driving and saw a spot where I thought that I might be able to sneak our small car into and leave for just a few minutes. I parked, but as soon as I got out of the car, a policeman walked briskly toward me, speaking loudly in French and indicating that I was not allowed to park there. There was no question that I was about to get a stern lecture or maybe even a ticket. I had to get in and drive away. In order to solve the problem, it was necessary to go out of the airport and drive completely around the periphery to get back to the road that led up to the main departure doors again. This took at least twenty-five minutes with traffic. Fortunately, MJ was standing ready to go when I finally did get back.

If we had known how difficult it would be just to pick up a paper that morning, we would probably not have bothered. The whole episode put me late getting into the lab and set the whole day back. I considered the Heads-Up to be more than trivial, although it was not a matter of life and death.

Another example of a non-trivial Heads-Up dream was one of MJ's. It was about her mother.

> **Dream of MJ, October 3, 1996.** *MJ dreams that her mother fell down in her house near the refrigerator and was unable to get up. She could see her lying there (Table 5).*

Table 5. Dream of MJ, October 3, 1996.

	Dream Event Fragment	Corresponding Waking Event
1)	...her mother...	Her mother was the individual that had the accident.
2)	...fell down...	She fell down.
3)	...in her house near the refrigerator...	She was in her house, but at the outer door.
4)	...unable to get up...	She was able to get herself up only after lying on the doorstep for some time.

> *On October 6, 1996, we went to visit MJ's mother who lived in another town about 120 km away and discovered that she had fallen earlier in the week (October 3, 1996). She tripped while letting the dog outside late at night and hit her head quite hard on the outer storm door. She made her close neighbour (who found out about it the next day) promise not to tell. She didn't consider it important enough to bother anyone. The dream alerted MJ to be concerned*

*that her mother might have hurt herself days before she
actually found out. The visit was made in order to see that
all was well.*

1) MJ did dream about the correct individual in trouble—her mother.

2) The misfortune was accurately depicted as *falling*, not being physically ill, or burning, or some other mishap.

3) While she usually spent most of her time at home, her mother did go out shopping and visiting and could possibly have had an accident somewhere else. While she was not near the refrigerator, she did fall. The dream was slightly inaccurate on the exact location of the fall, but it was at her house.

4) She was able to get up, but only after some time. She did lie on the step for quite awhile. Thus while she was eventually able to get herself up, she was undoubtedly quite distressed, as no one else was around.

This was certainly more than a trivial Heads-Up dream and alerted MJ to the possibility that something had happened. We did change our plans based on the dream and visited her mother. The true story of what had happened only came out after we arrived at our destination. Thus while we were alerted to visiting someone who might be in trouble, we were unable to stop or minimize the accident.

The question of whether a Heads-Up dream can be of any use to *change* the real-life outcome is a difficult question to answer. Here is a dream that suggests that it can be done.

> **Dream, August 18, 1979.** *Seems I am at the approach to a tunnel in heavy traffic and the SIMCA shows "hot." The next time I look, the temperature needle is right at the tip and suddenly the motor quits. I try to start it again.*

Having had a number of Heads-Ups go by, I decided to heed this dream and so I checked the fluid level in the radiator. It turned out to be quite low, lower than I had expected, and so I added water to fill it before leaving the house that morning (Table 6).

Table 6. Dream, August 18, 1979.

	Dream Event	Corresponding Waking Event
1)	*Seems I am at the approach to a tunnel in heavy traffic.*	Later that day, I am indeed in heavy traffic near a tunnel.
2)	*...the SIMCA shows "hot." The next time I look, the temperature needle is right at the tip.*	I look at the temperature gauge and it is <u>not</u> at "hot," but is in the "very warm" region on a hot day.
3)	*...suddenly the motor quits. I try to start it again.*	The motor quits and I try to start it again. It goes.

1) I found myself in very heavy traffic in downtown Nice, something that was fairly normal. However, I was in a new part of town and found myself in front of a tunnel. I

planned to turn left and take another street rather than go through the tunnel. Because the area was unfamiliar, I was proceeding cautiously.

2) Thinking of the dream at this point, I look at the temperature gauge of my second hand SIMCA car that I have bought. To my relief, the reading is in the high normal range ("very warm"), but does not indicate overheating.

3) As I focused on trying to make my turn, the motor suddenly quit. I quickly tried to start it again and did manage to finally get it going after several tries.

I do feel this dream was an important Heads-Up dream for me. Had I not added water to my radiator on this hot day, I might well have been stranded, waiting for a tow truck, in busy, downtown Nice. The fluid level was quite low and I added a lot of water. The motor temperature in this older car was still quite high, but the indicator stopped just below the danger level. The fact that I heeded the dream scenario probably avoided traffic disaster for me.

The following is a dream of a friend that most certainly was not trivial and, because she heeded the dream, saved her a very unpleasant encounter.

> **Dream of DM, June 14, 2008.** *I dream that a man enters my locked hotel room. I recognize that he was at the conference and attended the final party. He has dark hair and although he looks familiar I cannot identify him by name (Table 7).*

Table 7. Dream of DM, June 14, 2008.

	Dream Event Fragment	Corresponding Waking Event
1)	...*man enters my locked hotel room...*	The conference party she attended ended at midnight. Yet she was uneasy and unable to sleep. At 2:30 AM she made herself some tea. As she sipped the tea, the door slowly swung open.
2)	*I recognize that he was at the conference and attended the final party.*	I recognized the man as a conference member who had been at the party earlier. He stops, surprised that I was up.
3)	*He has dark hair and although he looks familiar, I cannot identify him.*	I yelled, "You have the wrong room!" He quickly left. I recognized him as the man with the dark hair.

This little dream was very short, but turned out to be quite important for the dreamer. She was attending a conference and had this dream the morning of the last day of the meeting. She went to the various talks during the day and, then, in the evening, went to the "wind-up" party and dance. The evening was fun and she had a wonderful time. When the party broke up, she went back to her room, which was in the same building complex as the party, and locked the door.

Unfortunately, she did not flip the safety latch. While she was very tired and it was quite late, she was uneasy, and unable to sleep. She made herself some herbal tea and was drinking it, when, to her surprise, the door opened and in the doorway was a man with black hair who had been at the party. She had not ever spoken to, or interacted with him, but recognized him as registered with the conference. He seemed to have a lock card or code card around his neck. While the dreamer was startled, so was the man. He seemed surprised to see her fully dressed and standing in the room and after she yelled at him, he left abruptly. This was a frightening experience for the dreamer, and she telephoned security. However, little could be done, other than properly locking the door, as the man had disappeared.

The dreamer had been unable to completely forget about this dream during the day, despite being very busy. Had she ignored it, the outcome very well might have been extremely unpleasant for her. While she did not properly lock her door, despite her concerns, she did not undress and get into bed. Although the exact motives of the intruder will never be known, seeing her fully dressed and standing, he probably changed his mind about attacking her and left.

Certainly, I am not the first to talk about dreams that seem to predict a future life event. Many writers and scholars have attempted to describe and explain this phenomenon over the years. However, none of the dreams that either I, or my small circle of friends and family have experienced are as dramatic or spectacular as those often reported by others. For example, people have reported dreams of being in car accidents or having close calls involving motor vehicles. Then, later on in the future, the dreamers were indeed in these accident situations and some were able to recognize the situation, remember the dream, and adjust their driving behaviour to avoid disaster. Other dreamers had dreams that family members or friends would have serious or fatal accidents. Sometimes there were several of these dreams with similar themes and outcomes. The dreams eventually proved to be accurate. A recent review of this area has been written by R. Van de Castle.

Such dreams are hopefully a once in a lifetime occurrence for the individual, but they undoubtedly motivate the dreamer to share the experience. Dreams of lesser impact probably are likely not considered important enough to mention. For example, a dream of meeting an old school acquaintance from another city and then actually running into them at the mall is unlikely to induce the dreamer to write to someone about it. Thus, the "disaster" dreams are often those that one reads about in books, and they are featured in many of the reports collected. However, important dreams like these do not portray the complete spectrum of Heads-Up dreams. Rather, they represent the most extreme examples of this phenomenon. The many thousands of dreams collected by Rhine, for example, often appear to involve life and death situations. The dreamer was probably motivated to send them in because of their uniqueness and importance in their lives. My dreams, and those of my family and friends, by comparison, are usually fairly mundane (thank goodness). Regardless of the subject matter, the patterns observed suggest that Heads-Up dreaming is present in our daily lives and can be used for our benefit and safety.

↔ 5 ↔

Heads-Up Dreams With
A Waking Time Delay

Thanks to careful note-taking I was able to keep an eye on dreams for months and years. Since many of the dreams did not fall into the Heads-Up category, I was interested in what possible information they might contain for me. Sometimes, reading a dream that was written down a month after it occurred will allow you to gain insight about it that you didn't have immediately after experiencing the dream. One of those insights was very helpful in my understanding of Heads-Up dreaming. While re-reading my dreams, it became clear that not all Heads-Up dreams occur later the same day. Some have a real-life corresponding event several days, weeks, months, and even years later (although, the decision to classify a dream as Heads-Up many weeks or months later can be difficult). What I looked for was a waking event that only happened rarely or even once in my life and that was related to a dream event that had only occurred once. This made it more likely that I had experienced a "delayed" Heads-Up dream. Here is a dream that did not seem to have any real-life corresponding event until five days later.

At the time of the dream I was living with my family in Paris. My two daughters were in the Canadian French immersion program and so they transferred to their same age grade schools in the Paris region nearby where we were living. While this required some adjustments, things were manageable. More problematic, however, my oldest daughter had been learning to play the violin in the local Suzuki program at home. We were having difficulty finding an equivalent program in the Paris area. We had enrolled DE (my eldest) in a school based music program, but the teacher did not like or recognize the Suzuki system and argued that she should be put with the beginners. We considered this to be unacceptable. Thus began the search for a Suzuki teacher in the Paris area. At one point we did find the name of several Suzuki style instructors listed and I spent many hours trying to track these people down. Most of them already had full classes and could not take any more students. Then, one teacher gave me the name of a woman that still might have room for another student. After many attempts, we were able to reach her by telephone. She did not immediately agree to take DE, but said that if we wished we could meet with her at the end of her teaching day, at a designated time, at a room in a building in Orly, a region of Paris.

This was my dream. It came after our telephone call and predated our planned trip to Orly to meet with the instructor. As it turned out, we were successful in meeting up with the instructor, but the corresponding waking event occurred five days later on November 12, 1986.

Dream, November 7, 1986. *It seems as if by accident we run into CM, DE's potential new violin teacher. She is in very good humour and grabs DE and tries to teach*

*her a little dance. There is a funny name for it. I am a
little surprised, but recover and ask if she was able to get a
space or time to teach DE, as this has been a problem. She
seems to indicate that it was no problem, more so because
someone else had quit.*

When I had this dream, I was very hopeful that it
would be a same day Heads-Up. I had become used to
getting a little help with my Heads-Up dreams and this
seemed like just the kind of dream that would indicate
that our problem would be solved. Here is the comment I
made below the dream when I wrote it down.

Comment (same day): *I get the impression this woman
might be the new violin teacher and that she will be a good
one. Sure hope that turns out (Table 8).*

Table 8. Dream, November 7, 1986.

	Dream Event Fragment	Corresponding Waking Event
1)	*It seems as if by accident we run into CM.*	After a frustrating day, given the wrong room number, we finally run into CM as she is leaving.
2)	*...ask if she was able to get a space or time to teach DE, as this has been a problem.*	After apologizing, I do ask if she can consider taking DE as a student. I explain why we are so anxious to continue with the Suzuki method.
3)	*She seems to indicate that it was no problem.*	She finally agrees that she could take DE as a student.

| 4) | *Someone else has quit.* | Apparently one of her beginners had just quit. |
| 5) | *She is in very good humour.* | She was definitely not happy when we first met. However, by the time we say good-bye, she was in very good humour. |

We could never have foreseen the frustrating day we experienced. Nor did anything exactly like this ever happen again. With the entire family, we arrived on the agreed day, checked with the building attendant and went to the room, but she was not there. We searched everywhere and asked again, but as the time went by we realized that she must be long gone or we had the wrong place. After one more inquiry, the attendant realized that the room listed on the chart was in error. However, she did know where this woman taught and took us to the door. Coming out of that door at a brisk pace, looking at her watch, was a woman with a violin case. CM had waited for us for over an hour and was definitely not in a good mood. She said that we had come too late and now she had to go. I apologized, explained that we had gotten lost and asked if we could drive her somewhere to make up for the time loss.

Despite the fact that CM was desperately late for another appointment, and quite annoyed with us, she was a very nice woman and we were able to convince her to give DE a chance. She agreed to at least hear DE play one quick piece. It turned out that CM was just getting her teaching career started and all of her students were beginners. She was pleased with the fact that DE had been playing for several years and was, compared to all the others, quite advanced.

While agreeing to be DE's teacher was certainly not her first statement following our meeting, after she heard DE play, it became clear from the expression on her face that she was softening. She then gave us her first smile and said "Oui." The dream statement of "no problem" turned out to be essentially correct. She did agree. The woman relished the chance to teach at least one student at a more advanced level.

One of the other reasons contributing to her positive decision was the fact that one of her young beginner students had unexpectedly dropped out. She mentioned this as a reason that DE could be included.

There was no dance and CM was definitely not in good humour when we first met. However, by the time we dropped her off, and she had had a chance to talk with my wife and DE, she was in a much better mood and even began to laugh with us as we drove through Paris traffic and got to know each other. So the final outcome of the day was that she was at least in a good mood by the time we dropped her at her destination.

This is an example of a Heads-Up dream that was not so trivial and it happened five days after the dream was written down. It becomes difficult, if the dream is not written down, to accurately remember what was dreamed, and easier to dismiss it as poorly remembered, etc. As the days and weeks go by, careful dream recording becomes even more important. Here is a dream that did not seem to manifest as a Heads-Up dream until seven months later. I am sure this was a Heads-Up dream as the event was unique in my life.

Dream, May 31, 1978. *I am with KR in a church of some kind. The building is small, like a one-room school house and the end is red brick that is quite old. I notice how the brick is crumbling. I hear someone say that the decay is the result of the Texans or the unwillingness and "cheapness" of the Texans (Table 9).*

Table 9. Dream, May 31, 1978.

	Dream Event Fragment	Corresponding Waking Event
1)	*I am with KR in a church of some kind.*	KR, MJ and I are in a church that was called Grey Presbyterian church.
2)	*The building is small, like a one-room school house.*	This church was built in the late 1800's and was of the same vintage and size as one-room school houses.
3)	*I notice how the brick is crumbling.*	The brick was indeed crumbling. The place was falling down.
4)	*..decay is the result of the Texans or the unwillingness and "cheapness" of the Texans.*	The decay was due to neglect. Some of the congregation refused to spend more money to repair the building and left. The church had to be closed.

While I was used to keeping an eye out for unusual dreams, there was nothing in my life that struck a chord for this dream when I had it and I soon forgot about it. As with many of my dreams, there was no apparent immediate Heads-Up component. Neither did anything happen within the next few days. However, one weekend, KR (my father-in-law) invited us to go with him to visit the church he attended as a boy. It was in a rural area and was built when there were far fewer people in the area. It was a small building that was slated for demolition and we were going to see if there were any artifacts or memorabilia left. The building had a red brick wall and it was falling down. There was a small auction to disperse the few items still remaining with the property. This visit was quite an unexpected activity for me. KR was not an active church attendee and neither was I. I had not heard of this church until the day I went.

1) While I sometimes went on outings with my father-in-law, KR, as well as my wife, MJ, this was a unique experience. The church was completely unknown to me and this was the only time we ever went to see it in all the years that I knew KR.

2) This old, deserted building did remind me of a one-room school house of the kind that had been used by a previous generation. It was quite a small building, but no doubt served the pioneers in its time and was the same vintage as several closed one-room school houses in the area.

3) The building was in poor condition and the red brick wall was crumbling on one side especially. The roof had been leaking badly and the few contents were being salvaged and sold at a little auction since the building was destined for destruction by a contractor.

4) The story of how the church closed was a sad one. When KR was still young, disputes arose over who would pay for suggested renovations and it split the congregation. Some members refused to pay their full share of the estimated costs. This inaction resulted in a lack of any action at all and finally resulted in the closing of the church altogether. There were no "Texans" anywhere to be found in this rural Ontario setting, but there were definitely some "cheap" congregation members. I did correctly dream about the reasons for closing the church, namely the unwillingness of some to financially support the building. (My apologies to all Texans. My waking brain actually considers people from Texas to be quite generous with their money.)

Thus, despite the long delay between the dream and subsequent real-life occurrence, I know of no other day activity in my life that had any resemblance to this particular event. It was a once in a life-time experience and I have never experienced anything remotely like that since. While this was not an event that I really needed to know beforehand, my dreaming brain had previewed this day's events for me some seven months before I experienced it. I was somehow provided with information that I could not have imagined.

Finding delayed Heads-Ups (as well as same day Heads-Ups) requires the careful keeping of dreams, which must be written as soon as possible after waking with the date on which the dream occurred. Also, the subsequent real-life event must be unique in some way and the dreamer must read carefully through old dreams a number of times in order to catch these corresponding waking events. In order to aid in this search, I kept a day diary as well, a practice I have continued to this day.

Over the years I have had a number of Heads-Up dreams concerning my career. They often involved money. One of the realities of an academic trying to do research is the fact that he or she must constantly be writing grant proposals to agencies, trying to convince them that the research program is worth funding. Unfortunately, the response of these agencies is often "NO." The whole process takes some 6–8 months between grant submission and agency response. It is quite a stressful, time consuming experience and the outcomes are quite unpredictable. As you might imagine, I had the occasional dream about getting or not getting grant money. Here is an example:

Dream, December 20, 1989. I am at a University function. A man (FN, a colleague) is talking with KT (chair of our department). KT has a list of all those who got grants this year. He tells FN, in a sombre voice that he did not get any money. I am in the background feeling bad and expect the same news. But to my surprise he says "You got one"; I am relieved (Table 10).

Table 10. Dream, December 20, 1989.

	Dream Event Fragment	Corresponding Waking Event
1)	*Department chair says FN does not get an NSERC.*	FN does not get an NSERC grant.
2)	*Chair says that I do get a grant.*	Colleague GG comes in to tell me that I have gotten a big NSERC grant.

1) I got the news on February 22, 1990. As it turned out, for this competition, FN did *not* get any money. FN often was successful at getting grants and this was a surprise to me.

2) I did get my grant on this occasion, although the chair was not the first to tell me. A colleague had also heard and came to tell me before the chair could officially do so—although he did tell me after I already knew.

It may occur to the reader that this was a fifty-fifty proposition, that I simply wanted the NSERC (National Science and Engineering Research Council) grant and just dream-guessed correctly. I would either get the grant or I would not. The probability of getting the grant was actually more like 20 success vs. 80 rejection. However, I have had more dreams than I would like over the years, suggesting that I would not get any money. They seem to have been quite accurate as I have no record of ever getting a grant when I dreamed I did not get one.

Another important connection to this dream was that in late January of 1990, a student came asking about a possible summer job with me. He was a good student, interested in my research and if I did not take him, someone else would. I had to decide within days whether to say I would take him, not knowing if I had any money to pay him. The alternative was to play safe and tell him I was sorry but I could not make a commitment at this time. I decided, based on the dream, to say "yes." If the grant had not come through, I would very likely have had to pay him from my own salary as there was not a lot of extra or alternative financial support at my small university. Although I had already seen many Heads-Ups go by, I gave a special sigh of relief when the good news came through. It is academically interesting to see Heads-Ups "come true." It is downright scary to "bet" substantial sums of money based on such dreams. I have made a number of major decisions based on apparent Heads-Ups (one only knows it is a Heads-Up when the waking event occurs) since that experience and they are always stressful. However, "knowing" what is to occur months before it actually happens can provide strategic advantages in a competitive world where important decisions are often made with limited knowledge of the future.

≈ 6 ≈

Dreams of Others

Having long been watching my dreams for signs of Heads-Up activity, I was curious about the possibility that I (along with my wife) was alone in this endeavour. I have collected the dreams of my wife and my two daughters over the years, all of which I wrote down myself. While my energy to do this waxed and waned over the years, I was able to collect some dreams from my children when they were young and had no particular interest in dreams, other than they did have them and their father sometimes asked for a morning dream report. One compelling kind of evidence for the existence of Heads-Ups would be the demonstration of their existence in young children. I reasoned that if children had these kinds of dreams, then it would support the idea that this is a normal phenomenon that everyone can do to a certain extent. When my oldest daughter was 6 years old, she awoke in the middle of the night and told me this very upsetting dream:

Dream of DE, July 11, 1983. We are at a party with grandma and grandpa R. as well as other people. I cry all the way through the party and everyone is unhappy.

Four days later, grandma and grandpa R. did come to visit and stay over at our house, normally a very pleasant event for us all. We decided to take the grandparents, my sister-in-law, and our own family out to a restaurant that was normally a hit with everyone. However, it turned out to be the meal from hell. We were seated in a section that we were not happy with and asked to be re-located. The waitress did so, but was not overjoyed at the request and showed her annoyance. There was some concern when we ordered a hot dog for DE that she would not get it (our waitress said she would try). DE began to cry, as she was counting on getting this food item. My youngest daughter was quite young. From her high chair she reached and kept eating her creamy dessert with her hands and would not eat anything else. Much of it went on her clothes. Grandpa was not too keen on his steak as he felt it was not well cooked. When the steak was returned to him after further cooking, he was still not happy. Grandma, after the first few bites, disappeared from the table. It was some minutes before we realized that she was missing and we had no idea where she had gone. Then, we spotted her outside the restaurant, in the parking lot, walking around. Apparently she had gotten some food lodged in her throat and was choking. To spare us all, she had decided to do her coughing in the parking lot, away from the table. Fortunately, she managed to clear her throat and returned to her place. Somehow we made it through the meal, only to discover a fairly substantial error in the bill, not in our favour. Truly a meal to cry over, although DE eventually did get her hot dog.

I think that despite her young age, my daughter had just had her first Heads-Up dream. While she was not aware of it, I was able to spot it and it seemed to fit our situation. The real-life event did have a time lag of about four days, something that was not, from my own experience, too surprising. Certainly, we did not have any other parties in this time period, just daily routine. The visit by the grandparents and sister-in-law was on the weekend when we decided to eat out. We may have had a more disastrous gathering since then, but I cannot recall it. While my oldest daughter was too young to understand what she had done, she did have many more Heads-Up dreams as she grew up. When she was eleven years old, she had the following dream:

Dream of DE, May 27, 1988. Our school class goes on a trip to Toronto to visit the "Tour of the Universe" at the CN Tower. FF gets lost and everyone is very upset about it (Table 11).

Table 11. Dream of DE, May 27, 1988

	Dream Event Fragment	Corresponding Waking Event
1)	*Dreamer goes with class to Toronto to see the "Tour of the Universe" at the CN tower.*	DE goes on a bus with her class to Toronto to see "Tour of the Universe."
2)	*FF gets lost.*	When the class is ready to leave the Tour, they cannot find classmate FF.
3)	*...everyone is very upset about it.*	The teachers become frantic after he is missing for over two hours. Security involved—general panic. FF managed to lock himself in an unfinished, off-limits bathroom in a construction area. He was out of earshot.

1) This dream preceded her trip with the school class to Toronto and she was very excited as it was the first time she had gone so far without either me or my wife being along. Since they did go to the Tour of the Universe in Toronto as planned, and everyone expected her to go, this part of the dream did not provide any surprises.

2) More exciting was the fact that one of her classmates, FF, managed to disappear for several hours. He went into an unfinished bathroom in the tower and was inadvertently locked in by a construction worker. He did a lot of pounding and screaming before he was found, some hours later. This was quite unforeseen by anyone as far as I know. She also got the right classmate. There were approximately forty children on the trip, and she was not particularly close to this boy.

3) This event caused a lot of anxiety for poor FF, who had inadvertently chosen a non-functional washroom. It also caused major anxiety for the teachers and the staff. Missing children in a large city is not a laughing matter. I felt that this event did cause everyone to be quite upset and should be noted.

This dream had a four day lag between when I wrote it down and when the trip took place. My daughter had completely forgotten the dream by then. When I pointed out to her that she had actually dreamed this scenario several days before, she was quite surprised, but then realized that she had indeed had a Heads-Up experience. As I had seen before, dreamers very often do not imagine that that they could have a dream scenario that would resemble a real-life event at some future time. However, once it is pointed out, they are quite impressed and mentally run over the dream, comparing it with the real experience. Generally they find it to be quite amazing and discover even more dream/real-life connections.

My younger daughter also showed the same early signs of being able to have Heads-Up dreams. When the family moved to Paris for one of my sabbatical study years at the University of Paris, VE was eleven years old and we enrolled her in the French school near our apartment. She met new friends and generally fit in well, but she also missed her friends in Canada. Her only means of communication with them was through the "snail mail" system as there was no email at that time and telephone calls were far too expensive to allow. The idea that we might predict even when mail would actually come was difficult. Predicting the number of pieces of mail, would be even more daunting. The mail, when it did come, usually consisted of the odd letter from our parents in Canada, updates from my secretary at Trent University in Ontario, statements from our French bank and bills. The children did not normally get mail. One morning VE reported her dream indicating that she would get a letter. Sure enough, there were two bills and one letter specifically addressed to her from her friend in Canada. Her dream was short and to the point and I considered it a Heads-Up dream. About two months later VE outdid herself. She had the following dream.

Dream of VE, November 6, 1993. *I dream that the mail comes and I get six letters.*

We excitedly checked the mail later that day but there was nothing. Worse, there was nothing for the next two days. Then, on the fourth day, she really did get five letters addressed specifically to her alone as well as a letter addressed to all of the family, including her. This was the only time in the year that she received such a large number of letters on the same day. Her friends had decided together to write to her and the letters all came at the same time. Once again, the appearance of this ability to Heads-Up dream is evident in a young person, suggesting it is a natural ability that needs only to be encouraged.

I have a number of friends, who, on occasion, have reported that they think they might have had a Heads-Up dream, but most of these are anecdotal reports from people who do not write down their dreams and so while I suspect they occasionally have these kinds of dreams, it is difficult to assess them. I have two friends that do write down and date their dreams on a regular basis and have done so for some years. I asked them to provide me with any dreams that seem to be of the Heads-Up type. Here is a sample from one friend.

Dream of FT, October 12, 2006. *My sister-in-law DI and I were shopping in Mexico. There were bright dresses and shoes, but they did not have my size. DI bought both dresses and shoes (Table 12).*

Table 12. Dream of FT, October 12, 2006

	Dream Event Fragment	Corresponding Waking Event
1)	*My sister-in-law DI and I were shopping in Mexico.*	To their surprise, the dreamer, her cousin, and their spouses were invited to a wedding in Mexico in November.
2)	*There were bright dresses and shoes.*	On the beach in front of their hotel, a vendor was selling brightly coloured dresses and some shoes.
3)	*...but they did not have my size.*	Dreamer hardly buys anything as clothes and shoes are frequently not in her size.
4)	*DI bought both dresses and shoes.*	The clothes and shoes did fit DI and she bought lots of both.

1) The wedding invitation came weeks after the dream was recorded. The ceremony was to take place at a resort in Mexico, and the number of people actually able to attend from Canada was small. The dreamer, her sister-in-law, and their spouses were able to go on this long trip with relatively short notice.

2) They had no way of knowing that there would be a clothes salesman directly outside their hotel when they arrived. She also correctly named the kinds of things being sold—clothes and shoes. There can be a wide variety of things for sale in Mexico, including leather goods, pottery, and so on.

3) The dreamer had no way of knowing that the clothes would not be in her size. She did not buy anything for this

reason, but she would have loved to do so, had there been something that fit.

4) DI did buy lots of things as the prices were reasonable and they did fit.

This seemed like a typical Heads-Up dream with a few weeks lag time. The dream was "just a dream" until looked at in terms of what happened later in her life.

Sometimes, Heads-Up dreams, for some reason, utilize metaphors. Despite this, there is also enough literal references to the real-life events for the dream to be confidently categorized. Below is an example of such a dream.

> **Dream of FT, March 5, 2001.** *I dreamed that someone wanted me to get into a truck. When the door was opened, I climbed into the back seat of the truck and sat on someone—a male. He was twenty-one years old; although, I did not know him (Table 13).*

Table 13. Dream of FT, March 5, 2001

	Dream Event Fragment	Corresponding Waking Event
1)	...*someone wanted me to get into a truck.*	Before her class, a young man had offered her a ride in his jeep.
2)	*I climbed into the back seat of the truck and sat on someone.*	She reprimanded him for his inappropriate behaviour.
3)	...*a male. He was twenty-one years old; although, I did not know him.*	The person was a young male and she did not know him very well, just as someone in her class.

1) My friend was teaching on this day after the dream and while walking to class from her parked car, a young man pulled up beside her in his jeep and offered her a ride. She remembered that he had been sending more than a normal number of emails and the first week of class had left a little gift for her on her lectern. While a jeep is not exactly a truck, I think the dream imagery is close enough to warrant a hit.

2) The term "sitting on someone" can sometimes mean reprimanding them. While she did not literally climb into the "truck," she did "sit on him" figuratively. She verbally scolded the individual on the spot. Despite the symbolic nature of this dream element, I considered it a hit.

3) The person was indeed male and young, about twenty-one years of age although my colleague was never able to ascertain his exact age at the time of this dream. Since this was the beginning of a semester, she had not gotten to know many of the students in this senior class very well.

Later that day, the dreamer came to see me and asked what this could possibly mean. Between us, we ran through a few possibilities, but could think of nothing particularly meaningful. It seemed like one of many dreams that go by and don't reveal anything special to the dreamer. I did note that maybe she was "sitting on someone" or reprimanding them, maybe in her class. Interestingly, she had not heard this metaphor before and could think of no connection like that.

The next day, right after her class, she came to see me again. She had just scolded a young man for being overly familiar in her class and was quite amazed at how this event fit with her dream of the day before. Since reprimands of this type are quite rare, I considered it a Heads-Up dream.

While the first dream could be considered trivial (the subject being shopping in Mexico), the second was more important. She was not only making herself aware of a possible serious problem in her class, but she somehow previewed for herself the general scenario that subsequently played out. What made this dream interesting was the fact that I had offhandedly guessed the meaning of her metaphor—although neither of us realized it until the next day. She, on the other hand, claimed to never have heard of, or used the expression "sit on him," although it is quite possible that she had heard it at some point in her life and forgotten about it.

What about romance? Are Heads-Up dreams useful in the area of romantic relationships? Like Heads-Up dreams in any other life situation, ignoring extremely upsetting dreams about an individual you are dating would seem quite unwise. For example, one woman dreamed that a man she had recently met would be extremely aggressive and physically rude when he arrived for their first date, although he had earlier seemed quite civilized and polite. The dream was quite right, and she suffered through quite an unpleasant evening. In another case, a woman had been dating someone for several months. She then had a dream that at one point he turned into a snake and slithered away through the grass. The "snake-in-the grass" symbolism turned out to be quite accurate. Very soon after the dream, his true character became clear to her and the relationship ended soon after.

Here is the dream of one of my friends who was looking for a life partner. This is a Heads-Up that she had, heralding the beginning of their relationship:

> **Dream of MN, April 12, 2003.** *I am on an elevator going up very high. I am with a friend and we get off on the 22nd floor. I notice that we are at the symphony, which is also a beach. There is white beach sand, warm temperatures, and palm trees here. A man comes up to me and asks me if I would have dinner with him—he has very blue eyes. I say "yes" and he is very happy. He says he was not sure I would because he is seventeen years older than me. I get on the elevator and go down to the first floor. A younger man is sitting at a desk and he too has very blue eyes. He is very sad.*

Her comments on this dream were as follows: I meet MV at the symphony a few weeks later. He has very blue eyes and is eighteen years older. Shortly after meeting at the symphony, MV asks me to have dinner with him. I was seeing a younger man at the time (also had blue eyes) but we did not connect well.

She commented on this dream again after her marriage: "We were married three years later on October 22nd (same number as the floor the elevator stopped at—I just realized that as I wrote it out)."

It is likely that many individuals have Heads Up dreams. The ability appears to be present at quite a young age and does not seem to require very much, if any, training.

⌐ 7 ⌐

Some Basic Dream Analyses

I have analyzed 277 dreams of my own (1970–2012) that I consider to be of the Heads-Up type. 107 of those dreams corresponded to waking events that occurred later the same day. 170 dreams had waking corresponding events anywhere from one day to several months after the dream, and a few seemed to occur over a year after the dream.

My percentage of Heads-Up dreams in the earlier years (before I stored them directly onto my computer) averaged 13.3% (1971–1992). The overall mean for the later years (1993–2012) was 11.2%. Thus, despite considerable variation from as high as 26% and as low as 0 for a single year, it would seem that slightly more than one out of ten dreams had a connection with the waking world that was unique enough that it could be scored as a Heads-Up dream. Figure 1 shows the number of corresponding waking events that occurred at various times after a Heads-Up dream was written down.

Time Between Heads-Up Dream and
Corresponding Waking Event

Figure 1. A substantial number of Heads-Up dreams had a
waking corresponding life event the same day as the dream.
However, a larger number of dream/waking correlations took
place between one week and twelve months after the dream, with
some occurring more than a year later.

I was also interested in what kinds of topics my
Heads-Up dreams were about. I categorized my dreams
into several main types. Table 14 shows the distribution
of the different types of dreams and how many there are
of each.

Table 14. The number of each type of dream and its relative
percentage of occurrence based on 277 Heads-Up dreams.

	Personal	Career	World Events/ Radar	Health
Number of Heads-Up Dreams	107	101	31	38
% of Total Heads-Up Dreams	39%	36%	11%	14%

64   *Head's-Up Dreaming*

Types of Dreams

The largest number of Heads-Up dreams I have labelled "Personal." These dreams encompassed a number of different topics including occurrences among family members and friends. The second most prevalent type of dream was the "Career" dream. I seem to have spent a lot of time dreaming about "yet to happen" events in my workplace. Interestingly, a number of dreams involved events and people that were not that close to me. I generally named them "World Events" or "Radar" as the information seemed to be available without my being aware that I was interested in getting it. The events tended to be about acquaintances or prominent media figures such as politicians that I had never met. For some reason, I was able to tune in to the activities of these individuals. Finally, a number of dreams were about my own health, but also the health of family members, friends, and my pets. The percentages of each of these dream types can be seen in Table 14.

Another way of looking at these dreams was to judge their relevance and helpfulness in my life. As already mentioned, these kinds of dreams, while they do appear to defy time and space, often provided information that would seem to be of very limited usefulness. On the other hand, they often contained important information useful to my ongoing life. I have separated the dreams into two categories: trivial and important, in terms of how valuable or useful they could have been (had I paid closer attention to them) or actually turned out to be, when I did pay attention.

Naturally, in the cases where I only noticed a dream/ waking correspondence at the time of the waking life event or after, the practical usefulness of the dream was small, even if it was important information. If I heeded the dream and adjusted my behaviour soon after I wrote it down, in case the dream had any validity, then they were often much more valuable.

The dreams have also been scored in terms of whether or not they resulted in a same day waking experience or a more time-remote waking experience. Considering all of the dreams, I found that 21 of the same day Heads-Up dreams were trivial, while 14.4% were of considerable importance to me. For the Heads-Up dreams that appear to have a waking event correspondence that was more delayed in time, 13.6% were judged to be trivial, while over 51% were considered to be quite important to my life situation. Thus, over half of the dreams examined were found to have a waking-life correspondence that was delayed in time from days to months to years and were considered to be very important. There was some indication, that the same-day Heads-Up dream, although easy to score in terms of its real-life correspondence, more often portrayed an event that did not seem to have a major impact on my life situation. However, a number of same-day dreams did seem to be quite important, and heeding them would have provided considerable benefit. Throughout the years, the remote Heads-Up dream has clearly been the most valuable in terms of career and personal life. Figure 2 shows the relative number of each kind of Heads-Up from 1970–2012.

I considered the possibility that the Heads-Up dream is a just a product of my wishful thinking. If this were so, I would expect that my dreams would have mostly positive outcomes. I would be dreaming about what I hoped would happen to me, since I am an optimistic person and for me the glass is usually half-full. However, it is

Trivial (TR) vs. Important (IMP) Heads-Up Dreams

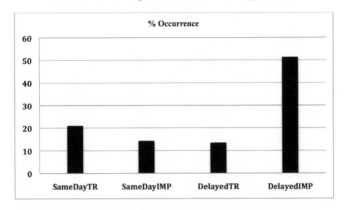

Figure 2. The SameDay TR (TR = Trivial) and SameDay IMP (IMP = Important) were dreams that happened the same day as the real-life event and were deemed either trivial or important. The Remote TR and Remote IMP dreams are those that had delays of one day or more between the dream and the waking event.

also possible that my dark side always expects things to be bad and that my Heads-Up dreams generally predate negative activities. I made up a five point scale (called a Likert scale) and rated all of the dreams in terms of their degree of pleasantness/unpleasantness. As it turned out, there were almost equal numbers of pleasant and unpleasant dreams, along with a lower number of neutral dreams that could not be classed as either positive or negative. A "1" on the scale indicates that the Heads-Up dream was about very unpleasant outcomes, such as the death of a human or animal. On the other hand, a "5" was assigned to dreams where, for example a very positive health change occurred in a family member or pet. A "2" was assigned for such unpleasant events as not receiving a grant or having a paper rejected by a journal—undesirable—but not life or death. An example of a moderately pleasant "4" event would be dreaming of receiving an award. Some events were given a neutral "3" as the real-life event did not evoke much emotion of any kind. Such dreams included those about someone that I did not normally interact with or see that much, but I did encounter later that same day. Figure 3 shows the percentage and distribution of these kinds of dreams. As it turned out, the number of pleasant + very pleasant dreams (36%) was very similar to the number of unpleasant + very unpleasant dreams (41%). 23% of dreams were considered neutral. I am always hopeful that my dreams will be a very pleasant, but I have long since learned that they can be just the opposite.

One of the things that occurred to me was that the Heads-Up dream might be somewhat shorter in word length than the non-Heads-Up dreams that I was having. While the numbers of these dreams are quite unequal, I compared a sample of 17 Heads-Ups over 3 years with a sample of 124 dreams that occurred in the same 3 years. A statistical T-test showed the normal dreams to be significantly longer, with a probability of less than 1 in a thousand that these differences were by chance. Since the length of my dreams might have been uniquely long or short for some reason, I collected a total of 30 Heads-Up and 30 non-Heads-Up dreams from friends, family and students. Each of the eight dreamers gave me 3–4 of their Heads-Up and the same number of their non-Heads-Up dreams. When I compared these two types of dreams for word length again, I saw the same result (Figure 4). *This means that in terms of recognizing a Heads-Up dream in the morning, having a very short dream could be a major clue.*

Pleasant vs. Unpleasant Heads-Up Dreams

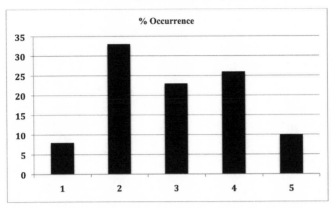

Figure 3. The graph shows the percentage of 277 dreams given a score of 1= very unpleasant, 2 = unpleasant, 3 = neutral, 4 = pleasant, 5 = very pleasant

Heads-Up vs. non-Heads-Up Dream Report Word Length

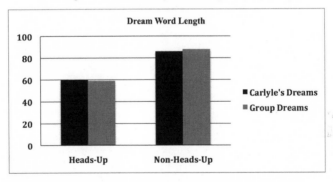

Figure 4. Mean Word Length of Heads-Up dreams. Comparison of my own dreams (Heads-Up vs. non-Heads-Up) and the same comparison of the Group's dreams. Non-Heads-Up dreams are significantly more "wordy."

There is a great deal of variability between dreams in terms of length, especially my "normal" or non-Heads-Up dreams. While the odd non-Heads-Up dream was as short as my shortest Heads-Up dream, there were many non-Heads-Up dreams that were much longer than my longest Heads-Up dreams. There are a number of dream researchers who would consider a dream report of less than fifty words to be too short to be considered a legitimate dream for examination. If I had adhered to this rule, I would have missed a number of Heads-Up dreams.

I would also venture that these dreams come at the end of the dreaming period, just as I am waking up and other Heads-Up dreamers have noted the same thing. I have a great deal of trouble remembering dreams in any case and must work on it constantly. These short clips are often the last and only thing that I remember.

In summary, more of the real-life corresponding events following my Heads-Up dreams occurred at least one day after the dream. In fact, the bulk of them occurred some months or even more than one year after the end of the dream. Although both trivial and important life events were portrayed, a much larger number of important events were indicated by the dreams at these delayed times. While the themes of these dreams were generally as expected, since both my family and my work comprised much of my life, it was a surprise that I had accurate dreams about people I barely knew or did not know at all personally. I always hope for happy dreams (who wants a negative dream?), but this does not necessarily result in a subsequent pleasant Heads-Up dream or waking-life outcome. As it has turned out over the years, I have had about equal numbers of both.

Content Analyses

Currently, one of the most popular ways of systematically examining dream reports is to utilize a system originally devised by Hall and Van de Castle. While the book is no longer in print, this method is now freely available online and includes scoring methods, sample dreams, and statistical techniques (The Quantitative Study of Dreams) with a website at *http://www2.ucsc.edu/dreams/*. The idea behind the method is to make the study of dreams adhere more closely to the principles of the scientific method. The approach is objective in that the dream report is scored in specific ways to categorize the content. The rules for categorization are explicitly described and, as a result, different individuals can independently score the dream report and obtain very similar scores in terms of categories chosen. The approach also allows for quantitative examination of the categories using statistical techniques. In other words, one can count the *number* of times that someone's father appears in dreams, for example. The focus is on the dream report itself, and no outside information about the dreamer or characteristics of the dream are considered; although, the system does require a large number of dreams to be examined. A scoring of the frequency of characters (men, women, friends, etc.), social interactions (aggression, friendliness, sexuality), activities (thinking, talking, running, etc.), successes, failures, scene settings, objects (cars, houses, etc.) that appear in dreams can be done. In an attempt to try to describe what normal individuals dream about, 500 dreams were collected from male and 500 from female college students. This set of 1,000 dreams was scored using the Hall-Van de Castle system and provides a set of norms that can be used to comapre the dreams of other groups or individuals. These norms are considered to provide a profile of the average dreamer. Some of the more important results of using this system include the fact that samples of dreams of any single individual are quite consistent over the years in terms of the kinds of things and number of each dreamed about. Further, the dream content is clearly related to the waking activity of the individual.

The dreamer need never meet the person analyzing his or her dreams and the the person analyzing the dreams need not know anything about the dreamer. A fairly accurate profile of the dreamer's interests, problems, and social life can be made by simply looking at these scores and how they differ from the norms. For example, there are many differences between male and female dream content. Male dreams contain more physical aggression than those of females. Females dream more about female characters, friends, and have more friendly interactions than males. Children's dreams have different content than those of young adults with many more animals appearing in the dreams of children under the age of ten. The number of animal appearances and activities decreases after this age to be comparable to young adults.

Because this method allows the statistical comparison of different series of dreams in the same individual, I decided to use it to compare my Heads-Up dreams with my non-Heads-Up dreams. My non-Heads-Up dreams are by far the most numerous and I chose seventy-five of them from my dream files that extended from 1970–2008. These dreams were scored independently by a scoring expert.

Although my non-Heads-Up dreams are of less interest, scores of my non-Heads-Up dreams were compared to the Hall-Van de Castle norms to see what kinds of differences there might be between my "normal" dreams and the Hall-Van de Castle norms.

Results indicate that I appear to dream more about food, miscellaneous objects, travel, money, household objects, and architecture compared to the norms. On the other hand, I don't usually dream any more than anyone else about nature, geographical regions, streets, indoor or outdoor locations, communication, clothes, or body parts. My non-Heads-Up dreams also have significantly less emotional content, instances of good fortune or misfortune and I dream less about failure, success, friendliness, or aggression than the norms. These scores presumably reflect my waking concerns and topics that occupy my thoughts, since one popular idea is that dreams do reflect waking activity. It is called the Continuity Hypothesis.

We also scored a sample of fifty Heads-Up dreams, chosen from different years between 1970–2008 and these dreams were then compared to the Hall-Van De Castle norms as well. More importantly, we then compared the scores of fifty of my Heads-Up and fifty non-Heads-Up dreams to see if there were any identifiable differences between them. We also took into account the differences in dream report size, since the more words a dream has, the more likely it will have a particular content item.

While my Heads-Up and non-Heads-Up dreams had many similarities, they clearly differed on a number of items. Most interesting was the fact that my Heads-Up dreams had less scene changes than my ordinary dreams. In dreams, there will often be a sudden change in scene as the dream moves along. My Heads-Up dreams showed less of this activity. Further, the scenes that were described were more often nondescript. That is, they were not clearly scenes depicting a room in my house or yard for example. There did tend to be more familiar characters in the Heads-Up dreams and the theme of success was reported more often. Events and items relating to travel were less likely to appear here compared to my non-Heads-Up dreams.

In comparing the Heads-Up (thirty dreams) and non-Heads-Up (thirty dreams) of the group, there were some interesting similarities. Most prominent again was the fact that their Heads-Up dreams, by comparison, had less scene changes. As with my own dreams, the dream locations were more likely to be nondescript. There were also more familiar characters as opposed to strangers or unknown characters. The group dreams differed from mine in that they showed more instances of indoor settings and did not show any differences in number of travel items. However, the number of similar characteristics of my own Heads-Up dreams and those of the group suggest that the Heads-Up dream has unique properties that can be objectively scored. Such a result, along with the knowledge that these dreams are often somewhat shorter than non-Heads-Up dreams, indicates that the dreamer has several indicators to guide him or her in deciding whether a dream is of the Heads-Up type. Below is a table (Table 15) of the Heads-Up vs. non-Heads-Up characteristics for both myself and the group, showing the significant similarities and differences.

Table 15. Most Salient Heads-Up Characteristics of Carlyle's Dreams and Group Dreams.

Carlyle's Heads-Up Dreams	Group Heads-Up Dreams
Dream length shorter than normal	Dream length shorter than normal
Less scene change content	Less scene change content
More familiar characters	More familiar characters
More nondescript locations	More nondescript locations
More success	More indoor locations
Less travel	

It is interesting that these two categories of dreams (Heads-Up vs. non-Heads-Up) could have so many content differences. It is theoretically possible that my dreams are not all that stable, although it has been reported that the dreams of a single individual are really quite stable in terms of content over the years to the point that they provide a sort of "fingerprint" of the individual's personality. To be absolutely sure, I compared a sample of fifty earlier non-Heads-Up dreams with another sample of twenty-five non-Heads-Up dreams taken from more recent times. Absolutely none of the content categories differed, supporting the findings that the dreams of the individual are indeed quite stable in terms of content over the years. The result also strengthens the idea that there are real dream content differences between Heads-Up and non-Heads-Up dreams.

These differences provide a way for anyone to recognize a potential Heads-Up dream among other dreams. First of all, it would be expected that the dream would be relatively short—somewhere around 50–60 words or less. It must be remembered that if the dreamer's "normal" dreams are quite long, the Heads-Up dream may be somewhat longer. The length is relative and unique to the dreamer. A potential Heads-Up dream is likely to show few scene changes, with a scene location that is probably quite nondescript. On the other hand, the characters are likely to be familiar. The group experienced more indoor locations in their Heads-Up dreams, but I did not. The elements of success and travel were only distinctive in my dreams and not in the group dreams. Thus, they are less likley to be reliable general markers to identify a Heads-Up dream. Overall, however, there is at least the beginning of a template for recognizing the Heads-Up dream before the corresponding waking event occurs. If these dreams are to be helpful, then being able to identify them soon after they have occurred is important.

⁀ 8 ⁀

Notable Heads-Up Dreamers

One day, about 15 years after I had begun keeping my own dream diary, I found a book by John Dunne entitled *An Experiment With Time* in a bookstore bargain bin; it was first published in 1927. I was amazed and delighted to see that this author had discovered and described the nature of his premonitory dreams just like I had been doing. Here was a very successful mathematician and aeronautical engineer, who had written a book in the 1920s about his dream experiences and had seen the same kinds of things that I was seeing. In fact, some of his dreams were much more spectacular than any of mine, and involved important world events. One such amazing dream occurred while he was a young man stationed with the 6th Mounted Infantry in southern Africa, serving as a soldier in the Boer war in 1902. Here is the dream:

> *"I seemed to be standing on high ground—the upper slopes of some spur of a hill or mountain. Here and there in this were little fissures, and from these jets of vapour were spouting upwards. I recognized the place as an island which was in imminent peril from a volcano. And when I saw the vapour spouting from the ground, I gasped: 'It's the island!*

*Good Lord, the whole thing is going to blow up....Forth-
with, I was seized with a frantic desire to save the four
thousand (I knew the number) unsuspecting inhabitants.
Obviously there was only one way of doing this, and that
was to take them off in ships...."*

Apparently the dream then became what he describes
as a nightmare, probably meaning it became very unpleasant or more unpleasant than it already was.

*"I was at a neighbouring island, trying to get the French
authorities to dispatch vessels of every and any description
to remove the inhabitants of the threatened island. I was
sent from one official to another; and finally woke myself
up by my own dream exertions...."*

Some short time later, a batch of *Daily Telegraph* papers,
along with mail for the troops arrived at their campsite
and he was startled to read the following headline:

*VOLCANO DISASTER IN MARTINIQUE. TOWN
SWEPT AWAY. AN AVALANCHE OF FLAME. PROB-
ABLE LOSS OF OVER 40,000 LIVES.*

In evaluating his dream, it should be realized that he
had dreamed about this event prior to any possible information arriving from the outside world. He had dreamed
of a volcano of devastating proportions, not a small one.
The volcano was on an island, not on any mainland.
While he did not dream the name of the island, he did
dream correctly that it was administered by the French.
He noted himself that he had missed a zero in estimating
how many people were killed, 40,000 rather than 4,000.

In actuality the figure in the headline was an overestimation, although over 30,000 people did die in the tragedy. The fact that he had this dream at a time when he was in an isolated area of Africa drove home to him that he had indeed dreamed of an event before it had happened and while he was thousands of miles from the site. This led him to examine more of his dreams to see if it would happen again. When it did, he next began various informal experiments to examine the phenomenon more carefully. He originally decided to set a cutoff point of two days for time after a dream that it could be counted as premonitory in nature. If the dream did not manifest in a real-life event within forty-eight hours, then it could not be counted. With this rule he did find a number of dreams that confirmed the fact that he could dream of future events, many of which were more mundane than the tragedy on Martinique. As well, he tested the phenomenon on friends and relatives, and got a number of them to try to have dreams about the future. Interestingly, he found that he had to prime everyone to expect to see some kind of dream/next day waking correspondence as they simply did not understand how there could be any connection. He described the slow dawning that occurs, with the dreamer first noting only one little dream/waking event connection and then, upon further reflection, realizing that a number of the dream events were accurately represented during the day.

Furthermore, as he continued to collect instances of these events, he realized that the arbitrary post-dream time for the real-life event to manifest was far too short in some cases. He noted that one of his dreams actually took twenty years to come about. He had had the dream when he was a boy and only realized its full implications as a man. This was interesting and demonstrates that if the real-life event is distinctive and unlikely enough, it can be considered to be a premonitory type of dream. As a young boy of approximately thirteen years, after reading Jules Verne's *Clipper of the Clouds*, he had the following dream:

> *"I dreamed that I had invented a flying machine and was travelling through space therein. I was seated in a tiny open boat constructed of some whitish material on a wooden framework. I was doing no steering. And there was no sign of anything supporting the boat."*

I have dissected his dream in the same way as other dreams that I have observed in order to show the numerous dream/waking correspondences (Table 16).

Table 16. Dunne's Flying Machine Dream.

	Dream Event Fragment	Corresponding Waking Event
1)	*...I had invented a flying machine.*	Dreamer had invented a flying machine.
2)	*...was travelling through space.*	He test-flew this machine himself.
3)	*I was seated in a tiny open boat...*	The machine had no tail and was roughly shaped like a small boat.
4)	*...constructed of some whitish material.*	The "cockpit" (my word) was a fitted structure like an open canoe, made of white canvas...
5)	*...on a wooden framework.*	...stretched over a light wooden framework.

(Continued)

Head's-Up Dreaming

| 6) | *I was doing no steering.* | After the first lift-off and then brief touch-down, the machine took off again. By the time the dreamer regained his composure the plane was climbing well by itself and he decided not to try to improve on the situation so he kept his hands off the controls. |

The fact that it took twenty years for his dream scenario to be considered a Heads-Up dream by the author was quite comforting to me, as I had been worried about the idea of trying to connect dreams to waking events so far into the future. While the odds of guessing the outcomes for any of the above events seems in the millions, the exact probabilities are not estimable and we must be content with the idea that the dream has a significant number of dream/real-life corresponding details and is a Heads-Up type dream.

Dunne notes that in a book he read as a boy, there was a picture of Verne's idea of a flying machine, and that it looked like a large boat, except that it had small propellers to hold it up. Further, it had no wings—a design that could not, in reality, ever work. Twenty years later, he was now an aeronautical engineer and had actually designed planes. He describes test flying a device. He managed to get it to take off. However, it then bounced, and startled him—but then took off again, climbing evenly and steadily into the air. He realized that he was not controlling it and so decided to leave the controls alone as things were going so well. This device, like all of his designs, had no tail, and from below looked like a broad arrowhead with no shaft. The plane, of course, flew with the point first. For the pilot to sit, there was a fitted structure made of white canvas stretched over a light wooden framework. He noted that sitting in this plane, looking out over the edges, felt like riding a canoe through the air. It is interesting that Dunne *did not* reproduce from memory, the picture of the non-functional flying machine envisioned by Verne. Instead, he dreamed a flying machine that looked very much like the one he would eventually design, build, and fly. Dunne's book has many more examples of his dreams and many are listed in an appendix. What makes his work convincing is that he recorded a large number of dreams and was able to assess the relative predictive value of these dreams because he systematically wrote them down each day before the real-life events manifested.

An experimental approach to examining Heads-Up dreams would involve the written report of the dream, with an unbiased judge or judges to assess the degree of correspondence between dream and subsequent real-life event. Ideally, there would also be a reasonably large sample of dreamers so that statistics could be done. While a detailed examination of a large number of dreamers has yet to be done, the careful laboratory examination of single individuals has provided some fascinating results.

A talented individual named Bessent was exposed to a novel experimental procedure. He was to dream about a future lab generated event. But the event would only be designed and executed *after* Bessent had recorded an eight night series of dreams on paper. The person generating the event had no contact with Bessent and the actual event was the choosing of an art print from a large print library using a complex system to assure that the choice was random. Three impartial judges decided whether the chosen print matched the dream narratives for each night. They decided that he had done very well with odds of less than 5000 to 1 that the dream elements could have been by chance. An even more elaborate second study was designed and the outcome was the same. Bessent was able to correctly dream the nature of events *before* they were even experimentally decided and certainly before their occurrence in the real world.

Gary Schwartz, a scientist at the University of Arizona, has written about a talented precognitive dreamer named Christopher Robinson. This man had been a police officer in England where he was able to dream such things as the exact location where criminals were hiding so that police could proceed to the area to capture them. Christopher wrote to Gary Schwartz and asked if he could come to Arizona from England to be examined. Schwartz was able to do a very sophisticated and well designed study with this man. A number of possible geographical locations were prepared in advance. The choice of site to be visited each day was only made in the morning just before the drive was to begin. It was randomly chosen and given to Gary only moments before the start of the daily outing and *after* the morning dream had been recorded and handed in. Since Christopher had never been to Arizona, he knew virtually nothing about the area around Phoenix. Yet the correspondence between the dream narratives and the subsequent daily events was remarkable. There were ten different outings, one each day for ten days, and not all went according to plan as there were unexpected roadblocks and unscheduled stops. Despite this, the dreams accurately predicted each day's travel destination and events with remarkable accuracy. The dreams were required to be matched with the locations visited and the activities that took place. They were scored by an entire class of seventy-eight college students who had not had any original input into the experiment. The correspondence between the ten dreams and the ten reported locations and activities was over 98% as scored by the students. The table (Table 17) below shows the amazing similarity between the main dream themes and the actual locations/activities that subsequently occurred.

Table 17. The Precognitive or Heads-Up Dreams of Christopher Robinson.

Dream Event	Corresponding Waking Location
Day 1: The primary theme was of "holes, lots of holes" and a "basin empty of water." He later dreamed of a bombing in London.	**Sonoran Desert Museum—** an outdoor museum in a basin that was once an ocean. Schwartz's favorite section had prairie dogs with hundreds of holes in the ground. A bombing in London also occurred on this day. Hit Rate: 8
Day 2: The main themes were "shops and workshops... fabricating things... metal."	**Tubac Artist Colony—**to a specific shop that had metal sculptures, with a workshop in the back. Hit Rate: 10

(Continued)

Day 3: The themes were "heads, lots of heads, belts, leather, jeans."	**Tucson Mall**—Schwartz parked in his usual spot at Dillards Department Store, which featured a large number of mannequin heads at the entrance. Schwartz purchased one of the heads, plus a pair of jeans. Hit rate: 10
Day 4: The main dream themes were "suns, mirrors, LCDs, telescopes, Mount Olympus, airplanes, hangers, a pitched propeller."	**Kitt Peak National Laboratory**—at the top of a huge mountain home to the world's largest Solar Telescope. They ate lunch at the nearby airport restaurant with hangers that had a large pitched propeller in front. Hit rate: 10
Day 5: Christopher Robinson dreamed of a "car with four flat tires, no 'mineral' oil, and cars stopped by men at a 'border crossing.'"	**Gem and Mineral Store**—had a car with four flat tires parked out front. En route, they passed workmen stopping cars near a huge water tank with the word "Borderland." Hit rate: 10
Day 6: The main themes included police, moving vans, road closed curving at a dead end, murky water, and dangerous ladders.	**Colossal Cave**—with its specific "ladder tour." They also passed murky water, and the cave ended at a curved road closed at a dead end. A moving van had gone up the road and got stuck; afterwards the police came. Hit rate: 10

(Continued)

Day 7: He dreamed of "dust, dust everywhere, including on the floor in a building, a court room, and a train robbery."	**Old Tucson**—a western theme park also used as a movie set. There was dust everywhere, including a room with a completely dusty floor. They also saw a courtroom and a large train that had been used in more than 100 movies involving train robberies. Hit rate: 10
Day 8: The main themes were of "space, space capsule, archaeology, crossing over a dry river."	**University of Arizona Planetarium**—a space museum including archaeology and pictures of purported dry riverbeds on Mars. Hit rate: 10
Day 9: Christopher Robinson dreamed of "parking meters, satellite dishes, a murder taking place nearby."	**Downtown Tucson**—Schwartz intentionally parked near parking meters and a huge set of satellite dishes. The next day, the Tucson paper reported the murder of an elderly woman in downtown Tucson. Hit rate: 10
Day 10: The primary theme was of "trees, greenery, crossing over a river, and an Army building."	**Arizona State Museum**—Schwartz and Robinson crossed over a stream to get to the museum surrounded by huge trees and green grass, unusual for Tucson. They also passed the Army ROTC building on their return from the museum (which was closed). Hit rate: 10

The results of this study are quite compelling. The hit rate of 10 shown indicates almost 100% correspondence between dream and real-life event as scored by the class of judges. Christopher Robinson accurately predicted details about landscapes, close-up features, place names, as well as unexpected changes in travel plans not described by the location cards.

❧ 9 ❧

Health Dreams

One group of dreams that especially intrigued me were Heads-Up dreams about health. The following is one of the first dreams I ever recorded:

> *Dream, December 1969. I am walking across a little bridge that seems to be made of logs placed side by side. As I step on them, I realize that they are large Rothman's cigarettes. Then, each log turns into a poisonous snake. One end of each log becomes the head of the snake and they bite me all over. I feel a poison going through my system. (I awoke feeling upset and a little ill.)*

As an addicted smoker, my first response to this dream was to reach for a cigarette to calm myself and start the day. At this point in my life, as a graduate student, I was smoking about 65–70 cigarettes per day. I did not consider this particularly unusual as my roommate also smoked over sixty cigarettes per day and many other students and faculty smoked well over a pack a day. The message about the health dangers of smoking had not yet gained much momentum and students routinely smoked in class, as did the lecturer. I am not very artistic, but I was moved to try to draw this dream experience (Fig. 5).

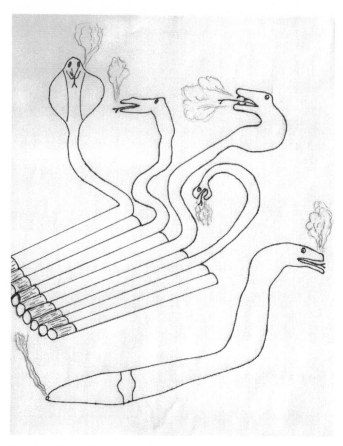

Figure 5. Toxic Nicotine Snakes.

Despite the graphic nature of this dream, I was actually able to imagine that it might not have meant anything important. Although at that point I was not sharing my dreams with anyone, I decided to ask my friend in the lab across the hall what he thought. Despite being a smoker himself, he snorted when he heard the dream. To him it was obvious. "Sounds like your smoking is going to kill you," he laughed. Interestingly, there was no sudden realization or insight on my part, even after this statement and despite the upsetting nature of the dream itself. I still actually wondered if the dream really did have anything to do with me—and after all, it was just a dream. In looking back at this event, I find it amazing that my reaction to this dream was not more insightful at the time—but it was not. However, I did decide to participate in an experimental "Quit Smoking" clinical project that was being run by a fellow student. I managed to completely quit smoking (despite a number of relapses) in the next two years and have never smoked since. With time, I began to realize that the dream (which my brain somehow presented to me) had provided me with an important warning about my health. Although I was actually looking for my dreams to provide some insights at the time, I was slow to recognize it when I did get useful information. However, that insight had instantly come from my friend, who hadn't read about dreams at all. I simply was not ready for my own dreams to bring me bad news. I indeed seemed to have a large "blind spot" concerning my filthy habit. Some would call it denial.

I was able to observe health related dreams in others. One of my patients asked me what the following dream might mean:

> *"I am at my future in-laws' summer cottage in front of a lake. I decide to dive off the diving board into the lake. I dive straight down into the water, but when I go to swim back to the surface, I seem unable to do so and fear I will drown."*

This patient was a woman in her early 20s who had a very slight build and could not have weighed more than 120 pounds. Because she did not fit the more stereotypical body type or age of someone suffering from sleep apnea, I did not consider it a likely possibility. Rather, I decided to pursue the possibility that she had committed to getting married and was now having some conflicting thoughts. However, she did not seem to think that there were any problems in this area. She felt that she got along well with her boyfriend's parents and was looking forward to the big event. Fortunately, some days later, she dropped by with another dream:

"I am a sailor, standing on a battleship. Suddenly, I am shot several times in the chest and I fall into the water. I wake up feeling short of breath."

Following this there were several very similar dreams, all having the theme of shortness of breath. As a result I reconsidered the possibility of sleep breathing problems in this apparently healthy young adult. A check at a sleep clinic confirmed that she did indeed suffer from sleep apnea (a sleep disorder in which the individual is basically unable to breathe and sleep at the same time). The addition of several dreams, although all somewhat symbolic in nature, allowed us to guess the true nature of her health problem.

The concept of a close correspondence between dreams and health has been around for a very long time, having been written about by such notables as Aristotle. Hippocrates, the father of Greek medicine, stated that some dreams had the potential to indicate diseases, humoral imbalances, or other physical conditions. Van de Castle provides a history of early dream scholars examining the relationship between dream content and physical well being. Dreams heralding a physical illness can be classified as "prodromal." These were dreams that portrayed a body part malfunction before there were any overt physiological indicators of a disorder in the dreamer's body. Dreams occurring after the disorder was diagnosed were called "symptomatic" dreams. The Russian scientist Kataskin considered dreams to reflect the dreamer's life condition. Further, he suggested that dreams were an indicator of the degree of physical illness of the dreamer. He argued that the frequency of the dreams as well as their unpleasant content increased with the seriousness of the illness. More recent dream scholars have supported this idea.

An example of a prodromal dream provided by Van de Castle was a recurrent nightmare by a woman with the following theme:

"...dogs were tearing at my stomach."

Several months after these disturbing dreams, she was diagnosed with stomach cancer. She died three months after the diagnosis due to this disease.

As to how prodromal dreams operate, it is assumed that the body condition, in an early stage of the disorder, is somehow conveyed to the brain before serious and advanced overt symptoms are observed. The early symptoms of the malfunctioning system or area are detected at some level in the body, are conveyed to the brain, and appear in the dream state to inform the dreamer about the condition. The area of the body and the nature of the illness are portrayed, often symbolically, in the dream. Intuitively it is easier to understand this kind of Heads-Up dream because it does not seem to violate time and space like many Heads-Ups.

Here is an example of a dream reported by a colleague. It would appear to be prodromal, but also had a Heads-Up component.

> **Dream, April 17, 2005.** *I see a female professor working at her desk. She is sitting in her chair and typing away at her computer. Suddenly her dress falls off and I can see a huge black and red bruise/gash on her thigh. She continues working and we continue talking as if this has not occurred. I look at the bruise and it makes me feel sick to my stomach.*

In interviewing the dreamer, I was able to chronicle the events that occurred in the days that progressed after the dream.

1) The dreamer sees a female professor and is puzzled by this dream. She guesses several other people in the department, when in fact the dream information is for the dreamer, herself. By the next week it is obvious who had the sore thigh. While the victim is not clearly depicted, a female professor (which turns out to be the dreamer) is described.

2) The dreamer was spending more time than usual at her computer and had an office chair that had been readjusted by another user such that it was at the wrong height for her. She did not take the time to fix it, even though it was uncomfortable—with nasty consequences.

3) As the days went by she noticed a pain in her back that steadily got worse. She did not attribute this to the chair at the time. Then the pain started to appear

in her hip and thigh and by the weekend, she could not walk because the pain was so severe. While there was no observable bruise, as depicted in the dream, the pain was certainly real and the final destination of this pain was identical to that in the dream.

4) She was not sick to her stomach, but she was indeed so physically incapacitated that she went to her chiropractor. The whole thing was an upsetting experience and it was several weeks before her health returned to normal.

This dream was of special interest because I was involved in trying to solve the mystery of the woman with the health problem. We suspected it to be of the Heads-Up type and we tossed around the names of several female faculty members and secretaries. However, the final outcome of this dream surprised us both. This dream is interesting because it has prodromal elements. The mystery woman turned out to be herself and the dream was portraying the problem that her sitting posture was causing to her health at an early stage. Her body was presumably signalling that she was having physical problems. However, it also had a delayed Heads-Up component in that there was an eventual problem with the thigh of the mystery woman, something she had no idea would occur until she had spent several days sitting in the uncomfortable chair. Interestingly, there was no dream portrayal about her sore back, which was where the extreme discomfort was first experienced. If, according to prodromal theory, the physiological signalling from a malfunctioning body part was indeed sent to the dream generator, it might have been expected that the dreamer's back would be part of the dream. However, the dream portrayed the final destination of the pain and apparently ignored the early "back" signals. The nature of dream generation using signals arriving from aberrant body parts must be very sophisticated, in that the dream portrayed an end state of a physical problem that occurred 4-5 days after the dream and ignored the intermediate stages.

In another case, DM was quite sick and was having health problems that seemed to get progressively worse. She had a number of dreams that seemed to describe problems with her intestinal tract. Here is an example of two such dreams:

> **Dream of DM, July 1995.** *I see myself pulling out all of my intestines. As I pull, the intestines get stuck in a knot and I am afraid that if I pull harder that everything (all my insides) will come out.*

> **Dream of DM, August 1995.** *I am in a hospital setting. I was unaware of why I was there so I went over to the nurse's station. I see a file on the counter with my name on it. No one was behind the desk so I opened it up and had a look. To my surprise it seemed that I was being treated for colon cancer.*

As the days passed she became very weak and was unable to do a lot of things that she normally did. She needed inhalers to avoid shortness of breath and was on several medications. The doctors continued to do tests on her, although they had not made any firm diagnosis. They had put her on an antibiotic that did not seem to be making her feel any better. Then she had this dream:

Dream of DM, September 1995. I get up from where I have been sitting and see that I have been sitting on the antibiotics that I have been taking. I examine the medication and as I look, it turns into a loaded gun.

On waking, she realized immediately that the antibiotic was bad for her and that she should stop taking it. She felt that she had to take personal control of her health condition and decided to stop taking the medication despite dire warnings that she would become much sicker. To the contrary, she soon actually felt somewhat better, although she was by no means cured. Her GP, wanting to rule out cancer, referred her to a gastro-intestinal specialist and in the next weeks she went for an appointment. The specialist immediately recommended exploratory surgery as he suspected colon cancer. This is not the kind of news anyone wants to hear and she told him that she wanted a few days to think about this and then she had the following dream:

Dream of DM, October 1995. A voice announces that I am allergic to many foods and that I must change my diet immediately.

This dream was especially clear and urgent for DM and there was absolutely no doubt about what she should do. At the next appointment, she told her doctor that she had dreamed that her real problem was related to diet and that she wanted to try to find out which foods might not be good for her. She did not want to proceed with the exploratory surgery. The gastro-intestinal specialist found this to be a ludicrous idea (not to mention that it was only a dream) and emphasized that diet had nothing to do with her medical condition. Despite this, she pressed ahead with both conventional and unconventional tests for food allergies and discovered that she was very allergic to many of the things that she was eating, especially wheat and dairy products. She avoided these foods, and her health improved dramatically over a period of weeks. She was able to stop all medications and discard her inhalers. She has, since that time, adhered to the new diet and continues to be in excellent health. Clearly, intestinal surgery would have been a tragic mistake.

The first two dream examples of this woman describe intestinal problems and suggest that the final outcome will be colon cancer. These dreams support the idea of a neural signal travelling from the pathological area to the brain to portray the malfunctioning body area, either symbolically or directly. However, the next two dreams are not so easily categorized. For example, the "antibiotic turns into a gun" dream indicated how wrong it was for the dreamer to continue to take the specifically prescribed antibiotic. The dream provided an evaluation, not only of the relative health of the body, but an evaluation of the drug as well. Further, the "diet and allergy" dream urging her to change her diet provided a solution to a longstanding health problem that turned out to be successful. It seems unlikely that signals from the intestine alone would be sophisticated enough to provide such a complex overview of the situation. Many of these dreams appear to have a Heads-Up component and a more comprehensive theory will be required to explain such dream reports.

It is, of course, possible to ignore or misinterpret these dreams. For example, Dr. Anita Leuthold from

Switzerland has described the case of a surgeon who dreamed (over an eleven year period) of parts of his brain having a tumour. He was interested in Jung and interpreted the dreams symbolically along those lines. He did not consider that the dreams might literally be portraying his own medical condition. He made detailed drawings of the "dream brain" as the tumour size grew in his dreams over time. He was finally sent to a doctor by his insistent wife—but it was too late. He died soon after of the brain tumour he had drawn so often. A more practical dream interpretation might have induced him to see a doctor sooner. Had this man, at an earlier stage, considered the alternative possibility that his dreams were literal "heads-ups" about his health, he might have enjoyed many more years of life.

❦ 10 ❧

Health Dreams About Others

While there exists the idea that internal signals from various parts of the body can alert the individual's brain to the early phases of pathology in the body through dreams, it does not explain how one person can dream about the physical problems of another.

A substantial number of my Heads-Up dreams have been about health, and surprisingly, many of them were about the health of family members, friends, or even my pets. It does not seem unreasonable to dream about your own physical condition, but I found it amazing to discover that I sometimes seemed to dream accurately about the health details of someone else.

The following is a dream that I had about an unknown (in the dream) female. I felt it was not a health dream for myself, as the dream character was a woman.

> *Dream, December 18, 2002. Seems that I am watching a body or body outline. The upper body of a female is filled with little dark granules... As I wake up, I am hit with the words "Folic acid," as if someone should be taking it (Table 18).*

Table 18. Dream, December 18, 2002.

	Dream Event Fragment	Corresponding Waking Event
1)	*Seems that I am watching a body or body outline. The upper body of a female...*	A female friend of mine had just had a check up. I only found this out when I called her about another matter
2)	*...is filled with little dark granules*	Her very recent X-ray showed little granules.
3)	*As I wake up, I am hit with the words "Folic acid," as if someone should be taking it.*	She was very surprised when I asked if she was by any chance in need of folic acid. She had indeed been prescribed folic acid in fairly high doses, to start immediately.

The dream has been dissected as always. It is important to understand that I knew virtually nothing about the medical properties and current uses of folic acid; however, I did remember that pregnant women were advised to take it. I didn't know who the female character in the dream was; although, I decided that this was not a dream about my own health because the body was female. I briefly considered the possibility that one of my daughters might be pregnant, but this was not the case. Since I didn't know who the female was, I checked out my more distant relatives and friends, but there was no obvious connection. I began looking up folic acid on the Internet. Later that day, a telephone call to a good friend about another matter, revealed that she had just had a check up by her regular doctor. The examination, which included several tests, *did* reveal some severe problems as shown by X-ray (granules). Hearing this, I suspected that she might be the mystery female and she was surprised at my asking if she might, by any chance, need some folic acid. Indeed, she had been prescribed folic acid in fairly high doses, to start immediately. I knew little about the medicinal properties of folic acid. Despite that, this valuable information was available from somewhere and I had somehow managed to tune in to it. This was a surprise to me and certainly the super-sensing prodromal theory was inadequate to explain how I might have done this.

In examining the Heads-Up phenomenon, it can be helpful not only to look at the activities of the average dreamer (such as myself), but also the talented dreamer. Fortunately, I have been able to get the cooperation of someone who has been using her dreams since she was a little girl and "discovered" the Heads-Up dream phenomenon when she was about seven years old. DM is a registered Cranio-Sacral therapist, but might best be described as a "Medical Intuitive." She has some extraordinary talents, especially her ability to accurately diagnose difficult medical problems. She has an estimated 10–15 Heads-Up dreams per week. In writing this book, one of my requests of her was to provide me with some Heads-Up dreams. Fortunately she has been writing down and dating her dreams for many years and has an estimated 11,000 of them. While many of them have yet to be closely analyzed, we found that well over half of them seemed to be of the Heads-Up type. She was, at one point in her life, a very sick woman. She solved her own health problems in a series of dreams mentioned in the previous chapter (imminent colon cancer).

Besides having dreams about her own health, she also has many dreams about the health and welfare of others. In one instance, an old friend of DM called from another city and mentioned that she was not feeling that well. She had what she called a "frozen shoulder" and it was causing her a great deal of trouble. Because of the limited ability to move, she found it difficult to do a number of ordinary daily tasks, such as putting on sweaters and tying shoes. Furthermore, things got worse as her other shoulder froze. She began to panic that she might have a serious neurological disorder. She had pain in her arms and neck and had been trying to remedy the problem for over a year. She had tried physiotherapy, chiropractic treatment, acupuncture, and had spent a lot of valuable time and money with little success. She lamented that she did not think that she was ever going to get better.

Several nights after the telephone conversation, DM had the following dream about her friend:

> **Dream of DM, July, 2001.** I dreamed that my friend was sleeping on an unusually large number of pillows and looked quite uncomfortable. Her head was way off to one side.

DM felt that the sleeping position of her friend was the problem. As a result of the dream, she telephoned the woman. After some pleasantries, she warned her friend that her next question might sound a little odd, but asked how many pillows she used to sleep on every night. Her friend was surprised at the question, but replied that she always propped herself up on at least 3–4 large pillows, the reason being that she was diabetic. She had had some bleeding behind one of her eyes about fifteen months before and the doctor had told her to keep her head elevated. The habit had stuck and she routinely slept with her head propped up. More recently, because of her shoulders, she was now also propping up her arms and a very complicated, uncomfortable sleeping position had evolved. On DM's advice, she decided to try sleeping with just one slim pillow. Although initially she had a few nights with less than perfect sleep due to the new sleeping position, the final result was excellent. Her back and limb problems completely disappeared. The remedy was a very simple and inexpensive one and it was solved by someone in another city that had correctly dreamed the nature of the problem.

On one occasion, DM was dealing with an older man, whose wife had brought him in for a consultation. He had received no satisfaction from the conventional medical world and so they were trying, in desperation, to see if they could get some illumination about his condition from DM. (Many of DM's clients come to see her after all hope of conventional therapy fails.) Almost immediately, she realized that he was very ill, indeed. The man seemed quite calm, however, and told her that he was not afraid to die. DM strongly suggested that they go directly to the hospital emergency station. However, despite this, he felt well enough to carry on with plans to go to the United States on a holiday that had already been booked. Unfortunately, DM was right in her assessment. The man died several days later while on vacation. DM felt quite badly about not being able to persuade them to go to the hospital and even contemplated discontinuing her work as an intuitive. However, in the days after his death, and before the funeral she had a dream about him.

Dream, January 19, 2008. I saw a man lying face down who seemed to be calling out to me. I am shocked that he has no arms or legs. I decided it would be best to turn him over. He looked right up at me and smiled. He was my friend's father who had just passed away.

As a gesture of good will, she went to the man's funeral. Some weeks later, she had lunch with the man's daughter and noticed that she wore a special little lapel pin. She asked about this and was told that the family strongly believed in donating body parts to others or to science when they died. She then mentioned that her father's bone marrow had been donated. Thus, his legs and arms had been removed and in the coffin, only the top half of his body was on display. It was not visually apparent that he had no arms or legs. DM had no prior knowledge that the man's limbs were missing and only found out at the luncheon. She then related her dream, and emphasized that the deceased was indeed smiling and that *he* seemed happy. The dream, besides providing precise information about the man's physical condition, gave comfort to a number of people. Family members were reassured that the deceased was happy and that they had done the right thing. DM no longer felt personally responsible for the man's life and realized that she had done all that she could.

The persistence of these dreams is demonstrated by the experience that DM had with her own mother. During the 1990s she had had over fifty dreams about her mother's physical condition and had repeatedly tried to warn her about the state of her health. A sample of these dreams is listed below along with the corresponding real-life events that occurred (Table 19).

Table 19. DM's Dreams About Her Mother's Health.

Dream Event	Corresponding Waking Event
May 11, 1993. Dreamt that a woman was showing me a book of interest. It was a book on women's health. It was called Our Bodies, Ourselves.	DM had never heard of such a book. However, a trip to the library proved there was such a book with the exact same title as in the dream. It was from the Woman's Health Book Collective.
Nov. 20, 1993. Dreamt I saw the same book as in the previous dream, this time the book remained open to a particular page relating to hormone therapy and estrogen.	At this point DM asked her mother if she was taking any hormones. To her surprise she admitted that she was. Her doctor had recommended it as a preventative measure. At this point she felt fine. DM pleaded with her mother to stop taking the medication, but her mother opted for the doctor's opinion and continued to use the medication.
Feb 4, 1994. ...my mother was in the hospital. Doctors were working on her behind a curtain. I pulled the curtain across. I saw my mother laid out with a large scar that ran straight across her chest. I noticed that she had no breasts.	DM voiced her concern to her mother following these kinds of dreams.

(Continued)

June 8, 1994. Dreamt that my mother was undergoing a surgical procedure and that her chest was being cut open before my eyes. I was very upset with the doctor and demanded that she be sewn back up immediately and that there had been a mistake.	DM again told her mother about these kinds of dreams.
Sept. 12, 1994.... I was at the hospital with my mother. We were awaiting her recheck following a medical procedure. I was told by an intern that it had been serious and could have killed her. She was being told that she would have to go on medication for a number of years. It felt as if it could all have been avoided. I was concerned about the meds. She seemed so frail.	Once again, she told her mother that she was continually having these dreams about her, but her mother did not, unfortunately, take DM seriously.

(Continued)

Oct. 9, 1994. Dreamt that my mother was trapped in a building and there appeared to be a fire inside. I was stopped from entering building by firemen. I was only able to look through a window into my mother's room. I was confused because I could see no evidence of fire. One of the firemen said "That's what it looks like from the outside, but inside, a fire is raging. It's just hiding." Then someone gave a signal to the others that the fire was located and that it was far worse than expected. It was on the top floor and moving quickly into one of the wings. Someone announced it was on the left side. I saw men running about in lab coats with something in their arms. They said, "We're trying to save the precious parts that haven't yet been affected. They are to be cleaned immediately, just to be safe. Now we have to go in and completely remove the whole left side." I kept asking how did this happen? A man said "We finally detected it because of the heat, now it all has to come out in order to get her out alive."

Although DM continually urged her to stop this treatment, in the end, her mother decided that her doctor knew best. She continued with the hormone therapy.

Her mother was then diagnosed with an aggressive form of breast cancer. She could not undergo chemotherapy as her health was too fragile.

They had to remove her left breast as well as lymph nodes on her left side because the cancer had spread.

Her mother was obliged to go on medication for five years after the surgery. She suffered from the drug's side effects and continued to have complications.

In speaking with the surgeon just prior to the surgery, DM was told that the cancer was estrogen dependent and probably the direct result of the hormone therapy.

(The surgeon mistakenly assumed that DM was a nurse and gave a lot of detail.)

There are many dream/waking event correspondences here:

1. Dreamed the title of a book she had never heard of (*Our Bodies, Ourselves*).

2. Specifically dreamed of the health dangers of estrogen in the same book. This book appeared in several dreams, open at the appropriate pages.

3. A dream led to the discovery that her mother was taking estrogen therapy as a preventative measure.

4. She had several dreams about medical problems in her mother's chest area.

5. The life threatening chest operation appeared in DM's dream.

6. The impossibility of chemotherapy because of her mother's frail health.

7. Removal of left breast and lymph nodes on left side.

8. She correctly saw the post-surgical need for strong medication which persisted for five years until her mother passed away.

9. Discovery from the surgeon that the well-meaning estrogen treatments were very likely the cause of the cancer.

The dreams clearly showed the progressive nature of her mother's declining health. The conclusion by the surgeon was relayed to her mother's doctor who had insisted on the estrogen treatment and this medical confirmation led to an apology. DM felt that this acknowledgment provided some comfort for her mother and for herself and aided in her mother's physical and emotional recovery from the operation. It also provided relief for DM, who was assured that she was not genetically predisposed to breast cancer. One can only wonder what path the health of DM's mother would have taken, had she heeded her daughter's dream warnings earlier.

⌐ 11 ⌐

More Health Dreams of Others

I am certainly not the first person to discover that one person can dream about the intimate personal and health details of another person. One author who described experiences where ordinary people have dreams about the problems of others was Robert Van de Castle. He wrote a recent review and history of precognitive dreams and has described a technique called the "Dream Helper Ceremony." Typically, the technique involves asking a group of individuals who know very little about each other to have a dream about one member of their group. This individual volunteers to be the dream target and is someone who has a significant, ongoing personal problem. The other members of the group try to incubate a dream for the individual concerning this problem, which remains a secret to all but the target volunteer. On the following day, the group meets again to report and pool their dreams. While no individual dream provides complete information about the problem of the volunteer, the collection of dreams paints a much more coherent picture. At this point, the dreamers try to guess what the real-life problem might be. Then they ask the target volunteer if he or she has any connections to these dreams. Remarkably, the dreams have similar themes and appear to zero in on current life problems.

I had the opportunity one summer to try this ceremony at an International Association for the Study of Dreams (IASD) conference. Along with about 14 other people, I listened to Dr. Van de Castle explain the basics of the ceremony and how we were to purposefully try to dream, for one night, about the problems of someone about which none of us knew anything. Our volunteer was a middle aged man who claimed he had an ongoing life problem. I had no idea whether I would be able to do this, but managed to get a dream that was somewhat unpleasant. The next evening, we all offered up our dreams and they were written next to each other on a whiteboard to be examined. Amazingly, there seemed to be a common theme of unhappiness. My own dream was as follows: "...a woman with suitcases and a little boy are walking away from a house. The woman is crying." As a group, we guessed some kind of unhappy domestic argument must be going on and possibly a marital split up.

While at first the man claimed that he was at a vocational crossroads—he soon broke down and told us that the dreams had hit a much more upsetting problem. He very recently had had an unpleasant argument with his wife and ordered her and their son to leave the house. This sad event had happened in the weeks prior to the convention and was still very much on his mind. Other dreamers picked up on different themes. One person dreamed that she heard a song that was playing on his radio. Hearing this song in her dream upset her a great deal, although she had no idea why. The man told us that the song the dreamer heard was the song that had been playing in the background when his wife and son had walked out the door and away from the house, while he watched from the porch. The content of these dreams quite surprised me. While I had volunteered to be in the group, I was a bit sceptical that this could actually happen and was amazed that I had actually dreamed details about someone else's life, especially someone I hardly knew.

Following the experience at IASD, I began to read about the Maimonides studies done in New York, that seemed to involve the transfer of information from one person to another through dreams. In these experiments, there were attempts by an agent to "send" the mental images of a randomly chosen art print to a target person sleeping in a separate bedroom. The person was monitored with EEG electrodes such that a technician could tell when he was in REM sleep and presumably was in an excellent state to "receive" the agent's mental images. At this point, the technician would signal the agent to begin "sending" the mental images of the picture. These studies resulted in some remarkable dream "hits" or correspondences between the chosen picture "sent" by the agent and images reported by the dreamer when awoken.

Considering the Maimonides studies and the Dream Helper Ceremony, as well as the dreams of DM, it seemed possible that one could deliberately incubate a dream about the personal details of a total stranger simply by looking at a picture of them.

This possibility was confirmed a number of times. DM related an experience that had happened to her some years before. While at a conference, a woman that DM had never met approached her and asked if she could help her daughter (who was not present). DM was not at all sure that she could, as she usually met her clients face to face. However, the woman later sent a photo of her young daughter by email. She decided to try and have a dream about this child and to her surprise, was able to provide very timely and helpful information.

Here is the dream.

Dream of DM, August 2008. *Dreamt of a light emitting from centre of the girl's brain. She complained of visual disturbances, nausea, headache and extreme fatigue. I was taking a sample of fluid from her brain. Possibly cerebral spinal fluid. It was clear. This seemed to be important. There was a discussion about placing a device into her brain.*

Then I was carefully attempting to fill a vile or test tube with this fluid. I had to put a plug back on top, which proved difficult because there was so much. Careful as I was, I did manage to spill a little. Someone said "Be very careful because this patient cannot afford to lose anymore." I saw a row of test tubes all lined up. Some looked as though they had been used for testing already, while others clearly looked as though they were still awaiting samples. Someone said "The first MRI didn't work because of the metal in her head." I knew there were more tests to be done, so I asked the doctor if I could assist. I told the doctor I had some medical experience and my hands were especially steady from my days as a dental assistant. I questioned why I'd even mention my dental background in the dream. I told her that I had a very special interest in this girl.

There was some discussion between the doctor and her peers regarding my assistance. I was eventually cleared. Then the doctor said that she would prefer an API 20 test. It looked like a small test strip. I agreed, not fully understanding what it was. She seemed to respect me and my efforts to help the girl. Later on in the dream the girl, her family, and myself celebrated with Chinese food (Table 20).

Table 20. Dreams for a Young Girl.

Essential Dream Event Fragment	Corresponding Waking Event
...light emitting from centre of girl's brain. Symptoms of nausea, headaches, etc.	Girl was diagnosed with pineal cyst (Pineal gland is photosensitive and located in the centre of the brain). Girl had identical symptoms.
Hospital setting.	Girl is admitted to hospital.
Problem with MRI due to metal in her head.	Girl acquired orthodontic braces days before the MRI scan. The braces distorted the MRI readings and a second MRI scan was required.
Took fluid brain sample which was clear.	Cerebral spinal fluid sample was found to be clear. No blood was present at the cyst.
Discussion about placement of device in girl's brain.	Doctors discussed the possibility of placing a shunt in her brain to relieve the severe headache pain. (Not done).
Some tests done but I wanted more to be done. Doctors ordered an API 20 test.	An API H20 test (unknown to dreamer) is used eventually to determine bacteria overgrowth.
Family and I celebrated with Chinese food.	Family celebrated the medical progress by having Chinese food. (Dreamer was not there.)

While DM imagined that this case was closed, she spontaneously had a second dream about the girl some months later.

Dream of DM, April 2009. *Dreamt that I was with the same fifteen year-old girl. I was in a hospital or clinic setting. In the dream someone was talking with a health care provider about the vagus nerve. There was an overwhelming feeling of exhaustion on the part of the medical staff and I felt that they had just about given up on her.*

There was only a discussion and review of the girl's symptoms. She was complaining about heat and a burning sensation in her stomach (Table 21).

Table 21. Second Dream for the Sick Girl.

Essential Dream Event Fragment	Corresponding Waking Event
I was back in the hospital discussing the medical condition of the girl again.	Girl was readmitted to hospital, unable to eat and extremely thin.
She appeared to be fading fast. Time was crucial.	Doctors were baffled. They decided it must be an eating disorder and considered sending her home with diet instructions. DM strongly urged the mother to demand further tests.
There was talk of a connection to the vagus nerve.	Further tests resulted in a diagnosis of gastroparesis, a disorder that is a direct result of damage to the vagus. (Gastroparesis has symptoms similar to those of pineal cyst disorders.) One of the complications of gastroparesis: bacterial overgrowth. An API H20 was used to determine this.

(Continued)

Girl complained of burning and irritation of the stomach.	Burning and irritation were two of the girl's symptoms

Happily, the outcome of this case was quite positive. Here again we see two dreams providing very helpful information. The symptoms of the patient were identified, as were the relevant parts of the brain (pineal) and nervous system (vagus). The dreams previewed problems with the MRI procedure, the doctors' discussion of putting in a brain shunt, and described the appropriate test to use for bacterial overgrowth—API H2O. (Actually the dreamer missed the H in the dream and called it an API 20 test. However, she was able to find it online and saw that it really had an H in the name.) Interestingly, while the API test name appeared in the first dream it was not actually carried out by the doctors until after the second dream, many months later.

However difficult it is to understand how someone can have a helpful dream about another person that they know, it is more difficult to understand how even a talented dreamer like DM could glean detailed, important health information about someone with only a photo for guidance. I decided to try an informal experiment with DM to see if she could do this again, with me providing the picture of the unknown person. This would allow me to ensure at least a modest level of control over some of the possible alternatives that could explain this seemingly impossible story.

To prevent possible information leaks, I used a picture of an individual provided to me by a colleague. DM had never met the person of interest or anyone in the family of the individual, but since the health situation of the person was quite serious, I decided to give it a try. While I had met the target, I did not know any medical details—only that the condition was serious.

DM was shown a group picture of 4 people because I had no single photo of him, but I hoped she would be able to focus on CP, the important figure in the group. Certainly the target person looked quite normal and healthy in the picture. I only knew that the person had not been well, but certainly did not know any more than the doctors—who at this point did not have a very good understanding of the problems either. The picture was given to her about a month before we met again to actually discuss any dream she might have had. When we finally got together to assess the dream, she explained that the night she had tried to incubate a dream about the figure in the picture, she did have a dream that seemed to her to be quite strange. She had no idea if it had anything to do with the boy in the photo, but she faithfully wrote it down the next morning, at 5 AM. She had this dream at least two weeks before CP was admitted to hospital. I have reproduced the segments that are clearly closely related to subsequent real-life events (Table 22).

Table 22. Dream for a Sick Boy.

	Essential Dream Event Fragment	Corresponding Waking Event
1)	...I found myself in a hospital setting.	About two weeks after this dream, my friend's son became very ill and was rushed to a hospital in Toronto.

(Continued)

2)	*There was a young man in the next hospital bed but the curtain was pulled so I couldn't see who it was.*	In fact the doctor was being very protective of CP and would not let anyone near him. He was behind a curtain.
3)	*He was being attended by a female doctor.*	She was a very ambitious female doctor with plans to include CP in her clinical trial study.
4)	*He seemed to be seriously ill.*	He had serious intestinal bleeding and removal of his intestines was seriously considered at one point.
5)	*...I was upset that the doctor was leaving her young patient unattended.*	He was often left alone and his mother had to keep an eye on him. He was getting sicker by the hour despite their efforts and she finally had to call the doctor to his bedside.
6)	*I had a sense that she (the doctor) did not know what to do with him.*	The doctor had ordered a double dose of the drug they were using. This was twice as much as he had been receiving and it was making him worse. Clearly someone had made a very serious mistake. Had CP's mother not read his chart when no one was watching and mentioned the possibility of a dosage problem, he would have been slated for exploratory surgery. Halving the dosage resulted in immediate improvement.

(Continued)

7)	...Later on, I was with this young boy and I took him to a gathering of sorts. I think someone said it was a healing circle.... Later he was showing me some foods...he kept talking about his diet and how difficult it was to find good things to eat.	CP was very interested in food and had taken up cooking after trips he had previously taken to Europe and India the year before with his parents.
8)	I think he had food allergies.	This fact had simply not been considered by the family or the caregivers. They managed to find a drug treatment regime that seemed to work and he recovered enough to go home from the hospital. In the months after this experience, he was tested for possible allergies and was found violently allergic to red meats.

I met with DM to assess the dream at the point that CP had been through his ordeal and had been released from hospital. I was careful to make no mention of CP's experience in the hospital or any comments about his health at all. It became clear after I read the dream, that she had somehow received some remarkable information from somewhere. She was not at all sure that she had dreamed anything of value. She had no idea that he had gone to the hospital or anything about the nature of his illness and was quite surprised to discover that she had been able to accurately dream about him and his condition.

Her dream did not just provide an assessment of CP's problem. It was a dream about a significant segment of his stay at the hospital, the social situation in the hospital room, the glitch in medication, as well as an assessment of one of the important health factors—food allergies. The idea that food allergies could play such an important role in CP's health was not considered by anyone at that point. In the months after the dream, DM did meet with CP and his mother. Subsequently CP was assessed for allergies and was found to be violently allergic to red meats. Up until that point, he had continued to eat meat of all kinds. Happily, he now avoids red meat completely, is medication free, and in excellent health.

The ability of DM to portray the health and future events connected with CP just by looking at his picture was consistent with her report about the young girl and was convincing for me because it was my picture and I could be satisfied that she had no obvious alternate way of finding out about the target.

≈ 12 ≈

Health Dreams by
Ordinary Dreamers

The dreams of DM for patients based on pictures alone were quite remarkable. Having experienced dreams about the health of others myself, I was curious to know if it would be possible for me, or any other average dreamer to assess the health or personal details of someone, just by looking at a picture of the person. Since I was teaching a course on dreams, I decided to have my class try to do something similar. I obtained a picture of an individual that I had never met, chosen by a friend. The woman had a problem that I generally knew was health related, but knew no other details. I showed the picture to my senior undergraduate class and asked them to try to have a dream about the health of the individual in the picture. I offered a small course bonus plus a lotto ticket for anyone who could provide me with such a dream. I also posted a reward of $20 for the most accurate dream having anything to do with the individual's real health problem. Unfortunately, the number of dreams that I received from a class of 65 was quite modest—12 dreams. However, a number of these dreams did seem to come very close to describing the illness.

The target was a middle-aged woman recently diagnosed with breast cancer. She was being treated for the problem at the time of the experiment and lived in a city several hundred miles away. Because of the preciseness of the illness we devised a number of content scales to be utilized. It was expected that the dreams reported before the students even heard about the project would be different than those after they were introduced to the project and saw the photo. Statistically comparing the elements of dreams before the beginning of the project with those after incubation of the picture, we found significantly more references to health, illness, and even to the exact nature of the illness. The probability of these results being due to chance was less than five in one hundred. Thus, despite the small number of dreamers that volunteered dreams, we found that some of the dream imagery that these students reported contained strikingly accurate images relating to the health problems of the target. Below is an example of such a dream:

> I was in a farmhouse atop a hill. The sky looked like there
> was a storm coming. I went to the kitchen and a woman
> was looking at me with a blank expression on her face.
> There was a knife in her right breast. There was no blood.
> All of a sudden I was in the hospital with the woman next to
> me on the bed. The doctor says the knife cannot come out
> because it would cause extreme bleeding. The doctor then
> said they could cut around the knife. The woman agreed.

While I was encouraged by these results, there were a number of alternative explanations. In order for me to conclude that the students had not somehow gotten the information from me, rather than the picture, it would have been better if I had not known generally about the target woman's health problem in advance. It was also possible that since they knew the problem was a health problem, they simply thought about some likely possibilities and then had dreams about characters with health problems. In other words, maybe just the suggestion that they should have dreams with health content in them was all that was needed and cancer is a very common illness. I decided to use this general experimental paradigm again and to improve upon a number of the features of the study.

In the second, better designed experiment, two dreams were collected from each individual before any mention of the project and introduction of the target picture. In this study, the entire class was required to participate as it comprised a part of their final mark. The target was, again, someone with a problem. This time, there was no rule that the target person specifically had a health problem and such life problems as money and relationships were also to be considered. Care was taken to make sure that I, too, knew nothing about the target person, who was chosen by a colleague. The target individual lived approximately 500 miles away in another city. A control group was given a picture of a non-existent, computer generated woman that looked very life-like and students were not told about this until after the dreams were collected.

After dream collection, when the nature of the problems of the target person were revealed to me, we designed a special set of items which might be likely to be dreamed about after the viewing of the picture if any of the students actually had dreams about the real target.

The target, a middle-aged woman, was described as having severe multiple sclerosis especially in her hands, requiring frequent medication to reduce the pain. Despite this problem, she was the primary caregiver for her mother who was in the final stages of lung cancer. At the time of the experiment, she was staying with her mother and administering medications. A respirator was available. The target woman, in her recent past, had also faced other problems. She had lost her husband to an industrial mishap. He was accidentally crushed by a front-end loader, and in the process, a limb was severed. More recently, she had had a very serious car accident. She was driving when she and her cousin were involved in a serious head-on collision. While the woman was not seriously hurt, her female cousin died of sustained injuries. Her son had also recently been involved in a car accident. Fortunately, while he was seriously hurt, he was recovering. This woman was now with her new partner and trying to put her life together again. Unfortunately, her partner was going through a messy, expensive divorce and the two of them were feeling the strain of bad health, bad luck, and shortage of money.

I designed a number of dream categories that I considered likely to be the subject of any dreams about the woman, if they were to somehow contain information about her life situation. They were scored using a modified Hall-Van de Castle content scoring system as in the first experiment.

- Torso/problems—any mention of torso or torso problems

- Head/problems—any mention of head parts or head problems

- Limbs/problems—any mention of a limb or limb problems

- Breathing/problems—any mention of breathing or breathing problems

- Other problems—any kind of problem not specifically defined above such as the mention of heart problems, cancer, etc.

- Financial problems—any problems specifically related to money or its shortage

- Domestic/problems—any activity or problems related to marital relationships

- Car/driving/problems—any activity relating to vehicles, driving, or driving problems

While these problems and categories might possibly show up in ordinary dreams, it was expected that they would intensify if the participants detected any of the problems facing the target. The category of "other problems" was added in case subjects somehow were inspired to produce dreams of any kind of health or problem other than those of the target. Dreams were scored using a graded system to capture the intensity of different categories. For example, for driving, 1 = reference to driving, but no problems associated with driving. 2 = mild driving problems (unable to control the car), mild car defects such as flat tires, etc., erratic driving considered dangerous and unwise, but with no consequences to the car or the dream characters. 3 = driving erratically or dangerously resulting in a car accident. Physical damage to a dream character or to the car. 4 = dangerous driving which resulted in the death of a dream character.

We compared dreams from sixty-six students that had seen the photo of the target woman with fifty-six dreams from a group that had only seen the computer-generated photo of a woman. This computer woman, of course, did not exist. Dreams were scored by two individuals blind to the nature of the experiment and the groups.

The results of this study were quite remarkable. We were able to score the dreams on the categories chosen and to compare the proportion of each category between Experimental and Control groups. Although scores that related to each category were found in the dreams of both groups, the most obvious difference was the intensity of activity. For example, both groups had numerous instances of cars in their dreams at the level of 1 (car/ driving involved) or 2 (mild car problems such as steering, small defects, etc.). However, the Experimental group had scores at level 3 (physical injury while driving) or 4 (death due to driving accident) far more often than the Control group.

An overall group comparison of all the combined categories showed the Experimental group to have a significantly greater proportion of 3,4 items compared to the Control group. The probability of this result occurring by chance was calculated to be less than 1 in 100,000. By contrast, comparison of dreams in the two groups before the pictures were shown was not statistically different. Figure 6 shows this result.

In all of the significant results, the Experimental group dreams had significantly more intense and more negative content than the Control group dreams. They included Limb problems (probability of occurrence by chance alone: less than 2 in 1,000), Breathing problems (probability: 1 in 100) and Driving problems (probability: 5 in 100.) Thus, there were clearly significant negative changes in dream content following picture exposure. Results of limb and breathing problems are shown graphically in Figures 7 and 8.

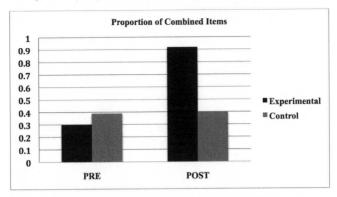

Figure 6. Proportion of "Combined" (all categories) items prior to target viewing (PRE) and after target viewing (POST) for both Experimental and Control groups. There were no group differences in content on these categories in the PRE condition, but for the POST condition, the Experimental group had a significantly higher proportion of all categories. (Probability of this occurring by chance is less than 1 in 100,000.)

Comparison of Experimental vs. Control Group "Limbs" Items

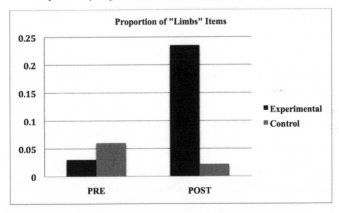

Figure 7. Proportion of "limb" items prior to target viewing (PRE) and following target viewing (POST). There were no group differences in the PRE condition, but the Experimental group showed significantly more limb content in the POST condition compared to Controls. (Probability of 2 in 1000 that these events could have occurred by chance.)

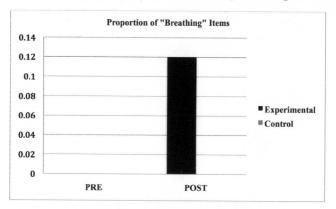

Figure 8. Proportion of "breathing" items prior to target viewing (PRE) and following target viewing (POST) for both Experimental and Control groups. Not only were there no differences between groups in the PRE condition, neither group exhibited a single score at the 3,4 level of intensity at this time. Similarly, in the POST condition, no items were scored for the Control group. Only the Experimental group had events scored in the POST condition and there was a significant difference between the groups. (Probability of this occurring by chance is less than 1 in a 100.)

Notably absent were significant changes relating to the "other problems" category, which could have included anything not specifically assignable to one of the designated categories. Such items as cancer, heart problems, mental illness, etc. did not appear in any substantial way. Although there were substantial scores for the head and torso categories, they appeared both in Pre and Post dreams. For the Control group, the dream content scores before and after seeing the computer woman did not differ.

For our Experimental group, who saw the real target picture, forty-eight of the sixty-six students in the class had at least one dream that fit into one of the three significant categories (limbs, breathing, or driving problems/activities). Eighteen students did not ever have a single dream about any of these themes. Of the forty-eight students who did dream about these topics, we placed them in one of the "poor" (11), "average" (14) or "very good" (23) categories. Students in the poor category (23%) did not show any changes in number of items in their dreams relating to the woman's problems after seeing the photo. While they did have dreams that could be scored as relating to the content, they did so as much before, as after seeing the picture. Students in the average category (29%) tended to dream more about activities related to the woman's problems after seeing the picture, but were not confident that they had done so and often felt that they had not (even though the dream content suggested that they indeed had done so). The very good group (48%) showed markedly increased dream themes and content relating to the woman's problems after examining the photo. This group was also the most confident and felt that their dreams were indeed about the target person. They often ventured a guess as to the nature of the person's problem along with the dream. Some samples of dreams that appeared to be related to the problems of the target are shown below:

> ...Woman (target) has crippled hands and can't open the pill bottle. The right arm does not work and there is a lot of pain. Her hands are all crippled and rolled almost into fists.

> ...Dreamer is driving. Target woman's husband pushes her into the road and the dreamer hits her with her car. The woman has an immobile arm. However, the man is dead. Somehow I (the dreamer) killed the man.

...a car hits my girlfriend and slices her neck open. She dies. (Dreamer wakes up crying.)

...I meet a family friend (woman) who tells me that her husband has died of lung cancer.

...I am in the dark and having a hard time breathing. I see people's faces around me. They are upset and I can hear them talking about me but I cannot answer. It is getting even harder to breathe and I am getting scared.

...It seemed like a funeral. People were going up one at a time to a casket and putting limbs inside. People were going slowly and putting arms and legs on top of each other.

The data suggested that many normal undergraduates were able to have dreams with content that reflected the real-life problems of an unknown target individual. They had only seen a picture of this individual, but it seemed to be enough. The content "chosen" by each Experimental individual varied somewhat, with each dreamer preferring to focus on one particular theme of the multiple problems of this woman. Interestingly, virtually none of the dreamers in either group dreamed about cancer or heart problems. Yet these are very high profile physical disorders that might be expected to be present in dreams anyway. However, such was not the case.

It is important to note the lack of any theme content when the target was fictitious. It is possible that the students involved suspected their photo of being fake. However, there was no indication that this occurred. All Control participants seemed to genuinely believe that they were trying to dream about the problems of a real individual. Particularly telling was the debriefing announcement by the experimenter (me) that they had in fact been used as a Control group and had not been dreaming about anyone real. There was a great deal of surprise, disappointment, and annoyance and I eventually raised the overall mark of the course by 2 as a reward to partially compensate for this "betrayal." Control dreamers appeared to have worked just as hard to come up with appropriate dreams for this assignment as had the Experimental subjects. In fact, students in both groups reported spending many nights trying to "get" a dream about the photo they were shown.

The security of the information about the targets was considered very adequate for the study. As primary experimenter and course instructor, I had no knowledge of the nature of the problems of the target individual. The pictures of the target woman, that I still had never met, were chosen by a colleague. She lived in another part of the country, and was completely unknown to myself or to the students. While a more perfect experimental design is always possible, it is hard to understand how the information gleaned from these dreams could have been discovered in any conventional way.

It is interesting to note that in most cases the subjects did not accurately dream about the exact nature of the problems of the target person in their entirety. On the other hand, there were elements in many of the post-incubation Experimental group dreams that suggested they were picking up partial information in some unconventional way. Of the four significant categories, individuals tended to have dream scenarios around one of these and not around the others. The reason for this remains unclear. Perhaps dreamers "chose" problems that most resonated with their own lives in some way.

Despite being treated in the same fashion as the Experimental group, the Control group did not dream more about imagined unpleasant problems after seeing the bogus person than they did before seeing "her." It occurred to me that they would certainly expect the person in the photo to have some unfortunate problem, since that is what I told them. However, their dreams did not become more negative in any obvious way. I concluded that individuals cannot be easily induced or given the suggestion to come up with dreams that would be acceptable to the project and/or please the instructor. The interested reader can find more detail in the journal publication.

⤙ 13 ⤚

Some Initial Theories—
Survival of the Fittest?

For many years, I found it easy not to tell anyone outside of my family about these interesting dreams. However, I realized that I was doing something that apparently no one else around me was doing and it occurred to me that I should be informing everyone of this terrific method available to help make both relatively mundane and difficult life decisions. I tested the waters once in a while with a colleague or friend, but did not get the warm interest I was hoping for, so I continued along in secret, hoping that things might change one day and I could talk about such activities without fear of ridicule—or worse, questions about my ability to progress in my job. I was very careful to continue to do my regular, more conservative research and reasoned that if I could convince everyone that I was a credible neuroscientist, then maybe they would listen to my more "far out" ideas. However, it became clear that as soon as I strayed from the path that everyone else seemed to be on, I got strange looks, uncomfortable postures, and negative comments. I managed to strike a compromise and continue in my career while recording my dreams as a hobby. Having an extra dimension to help make my decisions was quite helpful and for a while there was no paradox in using this information while at the same time teaching the status quo of brain research and latest information about the physiology of the brain. My research, which clearly implicated memory processing during sleep states was already controversial and was considered unlikely for many years by most scientists. It only became more widely accepted in the mid-1990s when other labs began to study the idea. The field is now considered "hot," and is still growing. Thus, I already had a controversial idea to deal with and the possibility that I would also describe a phenomenon far less believable seemed out of the question. (Of course, I had at least one dream indicating that coming out with a book or major paper on Heads-Up dreams in the 90s would be a disaster for me.) I heeded these dreams and acted accordingly. Little did I know it would be almost 40 years before I would decide to publically describe my experiences. I did manage to find a few close friends that not only listened to me, but began to do Heads-Up dreaming for themselves. I taught my own children to do this and they now treat the whole thing as quite a normal process in their adult lives. They have always paid attention to these kinds of dreams and used them for practical direction. Heads-Up dreams also seem to have helped those around me who paid attention to their dreams and had the nerve to act upon them. When I finally began to do presentations on the topic, I realized that a number of pioneers have already told similar stories and they have my greatest respect.

One of the prevalent attitudes of dream researchers to dream reports is that they are reflective of the past history of the dreamer. The brain presumably reaches into the memory banks each night and comes up with objects and actions from the past and puts them together to weave a story. Many dreams may be composed in this way and attitudes to this "story" vary from meaningless to profound. It is even considered possible that some dreams are simply a reflection of the consolidation of memories from the day's activities. However, biologically, it seemed to me that the body is also very concerned with survival. This requires that the most successful of us also look to the future. It need not be the far distant future but the immediate future, although both are important. The senses are concerned with so many immediate future things. Eyes are invaluable for making sure that we do not bump into walls or step off narrow paths. This is activity that predicts only seconds into the future, but it is obviously quite important. Hearing a loud motor as you are about to start across the street or smelling smoke in your house as you are about to leave for a day of work also helps you to predict what could be an impending disaster. In fact, the most successful of us are probably still around because we have sophisticated prediction systems that we have learned to use. Our five senses are all busy making sure that our immediate future will be a safe one. Further, our plan to carry out more long term basic manoeuvres like getting food, keeping warm, and avoiding potential danger are also done as efficiently as possible. In a way, we are organisms obsessed with the future, both immediate and remote.

Planning for the remote future can be more difficult. In looking back, it has always amazed me how often I had to make major decisions in my life based upon partial information. For me, these have included getting married, buying a house, choosing a career, making choices for my children, and so on. While logic and lists of facts, as well as the advice of experts and well meaning relatives and friends, are sometimes (not always) helpful, in the end, I have often made choices that certainly did not please everyone, and that seemed somewhat risky at the time. At a given moment, there is a certain amount of information available and on this basis, the individual does the best that he or she can. However, people don't always choose the right life partner, and don't always buy the right house at the right price. I believe that Heads-Up dreams can provide some extra input when making these decisions. It is tempting to postulate a dream system that works in the same way as the senses do, by providing advance information about a decision in order to aid the individual in making the right choices. Such a system would be quite adaptable and would be consistent with the Darwinian idea of survival of the fittest.

Broughton has suggested that psi abilities in general are probably an evolutionary product. Presumably the functions of such abilities as Heads-Up dreaming are there to ensure that the individual survives and passes on his or her genes to the next generation. This function includes the health and well being of the individual as well as the offspring. However, for many, the extreme physical struggle to stay alive has become less urgent, although it still may be part of the life of an individual. It seems easier to understand how Heads-Up dreams would be necessary during times of social upheaval when communication is unreliable and life and death situations are unpredictable. For example, William Bird was a Canadian soldier, during WWI. He describes how he dreamed that his brother (already killed in the same war) came to him in a dream and told him that he had to move immediately from his foxhole (although he and two other exhausted soldiers considered it quite safe and away from the action when they settled down to sleep). He awoke in a panic, heeded the dream, ran out of his resting place and toward an unknown site. As a result he lived to learn that the spot where he had just been sleeping had been completely destroyed by a stray bomb, killing the two other soldiers who had been sleeping in the same spot. Soldiers in his group had been sure that he was with the two others and were looking for any sign of his body or equipment.

Although less dangerous, survival on the highway is often a high risk activity. Many Heads-Up dreams seem instrumental in helping us avoid injury or death while driving. Ryback reports a number of dreams where the dreamer avoids injury while driving by heeding dream scenarios that depict the dreamer, or someone close to the dreamer being in an accident. Warning Heads-Up dreams seem to come to the forefront when it is necessary and appear to demonstrate a very important survival mechanism.

A proficient Heads-Up dreamer would have a better chance of survival than one who did not pay attention to dreams at all, although in relatively safe and prosperous environments, both the dreamer and the non-dreamer would be able to survive and do well. But over the long haul, the Heads-Up dreamer would be expected to have an edge because of some "advanced and accurate" information relating to the decision at hand. Thus, it is not unreasonable to imagine that nature has also provided us with a mechanism for seeing the probable occurrence of things in our lives that could help us not only to survive, but to prosper. I have used these dreams to help decide on a life partner, to buy a house, make career choices and travel decisions, and raise a family. If I had had a twin brother and he had not been the least interested in or utilized his dreams, I believe he would have had a more complicated and much less fortunate life than I have had.

The distribution of these abilities is apparently quite uneven in the general population, although it seems likely that most people can do Heads-Up dreaming. When I give a lecture on the topic, I always ask how many have had a Heads-Up dream experience even once in their lives, however trivial. About 50–60% of the audience put up their hands. In our North American culture, many individuals do not even pay attention to their dreams and so are unaware of the possibility. Many students have reported their first Heads-Up dream after I talked about it in class. Those individuals that I encouraged and mentored, improved dramatically once they put their minds to it. I have found that I am not particularly talented compared to those around me and although I have no extensive statistical data, it is clear that my friends and family members are better at this than am I, both in terms of hits per dream and frequency with which they have these dreams.

DM, for example, has a much higher frequency of personal Heads-Up dreams as well as complex Heads-Up dreams that are helpful to others. She uses her talents to guide her own behaviour as well as to make a livelihood. Genetics may play a role. In her own family, everyone considered DM and her mother to be talented in this way, but her father and six brothers and sisters were not so blessed.

On the other hand, I have noted my own ability improves with attention and practice. The number of "hits" in the first years of doing this was lower than it is now. While it is quite likely that there are definite genetic configurations that favour this talent, it is clear that one can improve with practice.

Can We Intentionally Have a Heads-Up dream?

Broughton suggests that it is likely that psi abilities in general are more observable when the individual needs something important in life. This seems reasonable, and many of my dreams concerned serious ongoing life problems. However, there were times when I had Heads-Up dreams that seemed genuinely to be of little importance and I have labelled them as trivial. Perhaps there was some important reason why I should dream a scene from a television show that appeared the next day, but I was unable to identify it. I even resorted to wild speculation in wondering about such events, but no truly satisfactory understanding ever emerged for me. It seemed as if my Heads-Up system was available and scanning, but had nothing really vital to relate. The result was just a sort of "test run" Heads-Up dream, to indicate that everything was working. Waggoner has called this kind of information "ambient." It is apparently information not purposely sought by the individual, and not of any personal interest, but available anyway.

If They Are So Helpful, Why Are They Not More Obvious?

Perhaps the urgency and necessity to utilize this Heads-Up skill is not as vital in our modern world. There is an unending source of information on the web to direct us. We can instantly communicate by cell phone to warn others of things that we feel might cause them problems or to call for help ourselves. There is GPS to track us should we get lost. And yet, the world is still full of apparently unpredictable events, often serious enough to result in injury or death for unsuspecting individuals. Despite our best efforts, our conscious logical approach to predicting the future, from natural events to world politics to economic trends, is far from perfect. Further, even when a prediction (such as a violent storm) is generally right, it does not always specifically relate to any one individual. I suspect you are still more likely to survive and succeed if you heed your own Heads-Up dreams.

A more plausible answer to the question is that Heads-Up talents would become more obvious if more dreamers kept track of their dreams. The many people who do not even bother remembering their dreams might be persuaded to do so, if they believed that some of those dreams would be very practical, helpful Heads-Up dreams. I am always delighted when someone excitedly reports to me that they have had their first Heads-Up dream.

Can Heads-Up Dreaming Abilities Compromise Other Survival Skills?

As pointed out by Radin, extremely talented individuals are not necessarily more likely to survive and succeed. For example, genius might be considered a distinct advantage in our culture. However, genius can be uncomfortably close to madness, and madness does not offer any survival advantage. The same might be true of Heads-Up dreaming skills. DM is an example of someone who is an extremely talented Heads-Up dreamer and is also capable of great empathy for the physical problems of others. Unfortunately she can literally feel their pain, a problem that most of us do not have. She spends considerable time trying to learn how to diagnose patients without experiencing too much pain herself. Thus, there is an unexpected, negative trade-off connected with her superior abilities. There would seem to be practical limits to these talents if they are not accompanied by other abilities and skills that are important for survival.

⪜ 14 ⪝

In Search of a Theory to Explain the Heads-Up Phenomenon

While I am not a physicist, I was planning to be a physical chemist in my early undergraduate years and took a number of advanced undergraduate physics courses—enough hopefully to provide a simple description of some the kinds of theories that exist. Most physicists are not interested in using physics principles to describe states of consciousness, and some do not like the idea at all. However, in looking around for theories to describe the kinds of things I have experienced and have observed in others, it is very tempting to look to the rather strange world of quantum mechanics. The odd and "impossible" behaviours of the sub-atomic particle world, and more recently, the molecular world seem just as bizarre as those of consciousness.

The Limits of Classical Physics

Classical physics probably shapes the belief system about how the world works for most societies and might even be considered "common sense." Here are some of the basic ideas: It assumes that objects in the environment are separate and independent from each other. (Moving one rock does not affect the others.) Furthermore, these objects exist even if you do not observe them. (Is your car there if you don't look at it?) The only way to influence an object is by direct physical contact with it. (If you want to move the table, you will need to lift it.) Time flows in one direction—forward.

Quantum physics was, by contrast, originally confined to describing the esoteric behaviour of subatomic particles that do not follow these "common sense" rules. However, the theory is now being used to best explain a variety of phenomena at the molecular and cellular levels, as no other theory seems capable. The theory has recently been used to explain such important events as photosynthesis in plants, the mechanism of smell in animals, as well as an integral role in bird and butterfly migration. This is a theory that seems to defy our "common sense" knowledge of the world. Interestingly, it is estimated that at least one third of the US economy is now based on technologies utilizing quantum theory. Here are some of the basic rules.

As measuring techniques have become more sophisticated and more precise, it is clear that the classical physics assumptions and theory do not explain all of the things seen in the laboratory as well as does quantum theory. For example, classical physics describes electrons as solid, discrete, negatively charged particles that move around the nucleus of an atom much like the planets of our solar system move around the sun. On the other hand, quantum physics describes the electron as something that cannot be completely defined as being in one spot at one time and can only be described probabilistically. There are, in fact, a number of probable locations of any electron wave form that exist at the same time (*superposition*) and these do not actually appear in reality. The exact position of the electron only exists as a particle in the real world when it is "observed." At the point that the scientist measures the system, the electron "chooses" a single location. Theorists (one faction at least) say that the electron wave form "collapses" into reality (appears as a particle) at the time of observation. The observer is apparently not independent of the electron he or she is looking at, but actually influences the outcome. There are a number of demonstrations of this, the double slit experiment being the most famous. In some experimental variations, conventional time seems to run backwards.

Another quantum concept is that of *entanglement*. It basically states, for example, that two or more particles may be linked so that any change to one particle is immediately exhibited by the other, no matter how distant they may be from each other. Because the particles do not have to touch, the effect is considered to be *nonlocal*. Such results have been observed in both subatomic particles and larger molecular substances. The change is instantaneous. This picture of the world is quite different than the one most of us carry around with us.

In summary, according to quantum theory, we are not independent from the objects that we observe and our expectations influence what we will see. Further, entangled objects are not independent of each other and changes in one object are reflected in instantaneous changes in the other object. The distance between the objects is not important and they can be quite far apart. Conventional time appears to run backwards on occasion.

One of the complaints about precognitive dreaming is the fact that it appears to defy the rules of classical physics—rules that are ingrained in our academic system and culture. Heads-Up dreaming flies in the face of our expectations based on everyday experiences and the many rules we have learned about reality. However, seen in the light of quantum theories, Heads-Up dreaming might not seem so "unnatural."

Quantum Theories and Psi Phenomena

Several main theories dealing with psi data have been inspired by quantum mechanics and are described by Radin. As noted by Radin, while quantum mechanics was not originally designed to explain consciousness phenomena, its stranger aspects seem more compatible with psi phenomena than any other theory. They include the following:

Observational Theory. The main idea is as follows: *The act of observing a quantum event probabilistically influences its outcome*. This theory became the first to predict and confirm that the observer influences the outcome as well as demonstrating a seemingly impossible time-reversed effect. One of the experimental demonstrations involved a computer randomly putting bits (1s and 0s) onto a computer disk. Normally of course, one would expect to find 50% of the bits to be 0s and 50% to be 1s. Since no one had yet actually observed the disk to see how many bits of each kind were there, the number of each was considered to be in "superposition," or potential states. Only *after* being observed, would they "collapse" into actual real bits on the disk. If the person asked to observe or count the number of 0s and 1s was asked to mentally expect more 0s, then, when the counting was subsequently done, statistically more 0s were actually found. Similarly, if the observer expected or "tried" for more 1s, there was statistically more 1s. An example from a psychology lab is one of a number of experiments done by Bem. Subjects were asked to try to predict which of two windows would open to show an erotic picture. *After* they had chosen a window, a computer then randomly chose which of the windows would be the one to show the picture. The subjects were able to "choose" the correct window statistically above chance levels—hard to explain in classical terms, but not in quantum terms. The final result was simply in superposition until a decision was made by the observer. Time was not actually violated; it just seemed that this was the case.

Weak Quantum Theory. This is an approach that is based upon the idea of *entanglement*. In particle physics it is required that particles have interacted with each other at some point. Otherwise, they have not had a chance to become entangled. In order for this to happen at the complex human level, a condition of generalized entanglement or non-locality is proposed to exist in nature. It is argued that all particles in the cosmos have interacted with each other since the time of the "big bang" and are therefore entangled. An example of this weak-quantum theory in action would be dreaming about the intimate details of someone else. The assumption is that there are entangled mental states due to shared conscious and unconscious activity.

Bohm's Implicate/Explicate Order. At one level, it is assumed that there exists a deeper reality, where everything is entangled. This level of reality is named the *implicate* order. Ordinary world observations emerge out of the implicate order and have been named the *explicate* order. The hologram is used as a metaphor to describe this idea, and the concept of reality as a quantum hologram has been considered by several authors.

Stapp-von Neumann Theory. In classical physics, the brain is considered to be a physical object with working parts and "mind" is believed to be an epiphenomenon, with consciousness only an illusion. By contrast, the Stapp-von Neumann theory deals with the "mind" problem by introducing the concept of the mind/brain. This approach allows the neural structure of the brain complete with axons, dendrites, and transmitters to co-exist with mind. Conventionally, the axons in the entire nervous system are believed to communicate by electrochemical means. That is, an electrical current travels down the axon and when it reaches the end (synaptic cleft), it induces an influx of calcium ions. If the signal is of sufficient strength and enough calcium ions enter, then a transmitter substance is released which induces a current in a neighbouring neuron. This current, in turn, will either activate (excitatory) or supress (inhibitory) the neighbouring neuron to fire. Stapp-von Neumann theory suggests that there is quantum uncertainty about the ion's exact location and that it exists as a clouds of potentials (superposition) instead of classical particles at specific locations. These probability clouds, observed by the brain, collapse into particles through the process of quantum *decoherence* at one synaptic cleft as opposed to another. There are a very large number of synapses in the brain and they suggest that the mind is needed to direct this large number of possible states of consciousness into one focussed state. This process is considered to be non-local, which further qualifies the theory to explain psi phenomena as well as

Head's-Up Dreaming

conventional activity. In this same vein, another group has proposed that the quantum mechanism is based on the microtubules of neurons, and they also suggest that the brain/mind is a quantum device.

Remote Viewing Theory

One group has developed a theory that explains a phenomenon very similar to Heads-Up or precognitive dreaming. They claim that their theory satisfies all the rules of physics and allows for the description of "normal" activity as well as psi phenomena. It was designed to explain a phenomenon known as *remote viewing*. For example, a person is asked to try to imagine the location of another individual. The target individual could be several or many miles away and the location could be a desert or a city street. Some people are very good at "mentally" imaging where the target is physically located and can describe and draw the environment. Even more interesting, the person can also successfully imagine where the target will be at some future time, such as 4 PM tomorrow afternoon. There is quite a formidable argument for the likelihood that remote viewing works with odds of 33 million to 1 that the results observed in 653 trials were due to chance alone.

Of particular interest here is the mathematical description of precognitive events, where the individual can experience the event before its real-life manifestation. This theory is able to explain the remote viewing effect and takes into account the possibility of remote viewing at a distance as well as remote viewing *prior* to the real-life event. For example, they suggest that the precognitive dream is *caused* by the subsequent real-life event as a result of time reversal. In this situation, the future *affects* the past.

On the other hand, they do not believe that a future event can *change* the past. Nothing in the future can change something that has happened and is known and agreed upon. Although one can see information from the past, there is no possibility for intervention.

How do they explain the degree of flexibility with precognition? Here is an example:

> One dreams of being on a plane and the plane crashes. The next day the individual decides not to take the flight. Later that day the flight does crash. They explain this very typical scenario as follows: The individual dreams about the real crash (precognition) and then dramatizes the event to include him or herself in it. Later, after waking, the dreamer can choose not to take the plane and avoid disaster.

It is a theory that satisfies the rules of quantum mechanics, such as nonlocality and superposition while also being consistent with classical physics principles. On the other hand, it does not detail how information from one individual could be transferred to another. It is strictly a mathematical theory and there is no discussion of neurons or parts of the brain. It is also difficult to understand how this explanation can adequately explain the waking discrepancies that are sometimes possible for the dreamer, such as in the warning dream above. If the waking event simply projects backwards in time, should it not then provide a dream that is a faithful reproduction of the waking event? This is most often not the case. As mentioned before, the Heads-Up dream provides a very good approximation (sometimes symbolic), but very seldom a perfect description of the future event.

Elements of a Satisfactory Theory

Any theory that attempts to explain the Heads-Up dreaming effect must be able to describe a number of phenomena connected with these kinds of dreams:

1. It must be able to explain the fact that the Heads-Up dream appears to defy conventional time by preceding the real-life event, sometimes by months or longer.

2. It must explain why Heads-Up dreams appear to be independent of space since they can be about events that are physically quite distant from the dreamer.

3. How can Heads-Up dreams portray the physical and mental conditions of other individuals, including close friends and family as well as complete strangers?

4. Why is the Heads-Up dream not identical to the subsequent waking event? An examination of Heads-Up dreams, even with virtually no symbolic component, suggests that the mental scenario is an approximation of the waking event, but there are almost always small discrepancies.

A Tentative Heads-Up Theory

In trying to create a theory to explain the Heads-Up phenomenon, one possibility is that there is a life scenario for each of us already scripted. This idea is not new and is the cornerstone of several philosophies. In his experiments with dreamer CR, Gary Schwartz was amazed to find that his experimental dream subject was able to provide a dream description of the next days' events prior to their occurrence. This very careful experiment led him to suggest that we are part of a pre-organized process and that the Universe is not random, nor does it proceed in a random way. His data suggest the existence of a universe with some kind of intelligent design. CR clearly "saw" a non-random future. This leads to one of the most salient properties of the Heads-Up phenomenon: it seems to describe (with a greater or lesser level of accuracy) waking events that occur at a later time. The time of occurrence of the waking event can be variable and somewhat unpredictable (although in this study it was always the same day as the dream), but the dream scenario always comes first in time.

One of the basic tenets of the theory I wish to propose is based on the assumption that waking events pre-exist in some state. The waking event has not yet been observed in the real world, but it is in a form that probably will eventually occur in the real world. If this idea is true, then how do dreamers access this material? While conventional classical physics does not allow us to ignore time and space as Heads-Ups seem to do, there are rules in quantum mechanics which might better lend themselves to explaining how the Heads-Up dream is possible.

Below are a number of hypotheses based on this idea, with an eye to the principles of quantum theory:

1) Waking events exist as one or more probable states (superposition) prior to their being observed in the real world. At some point, there is a "collapse" of one of these states such that the event manifests in the real

world. This idea suggests that at some point in time, certain life events have a high probability of manifesting in the real world. If the individual does not change his or her behaviour, then the Heads-Up scenario will likely become a waking event. Before this time, the event may not have such a high probability of actualization.

2) The dream state is especially suited to actually observing the possible potential outcomes relating to the dreamer's life. How the dreamer actually accesses this information is not known, but external sensory input ceases during sleep, and especially during REM sleep. This state would provide favourable conditions for the brain to pick up information and leave a dream impression without the competing sensory noise of the waking state. Since there might be an enormous number of individuals and their probable future events available, some focussing mechanism (such as attention) must be at work (a mechanism similar to being able to hear your name mentioned amid the noise of a loud party).

3) The reason that the dream event precedes the real-life event of the dreamer, is because the brain somehow has access to probable (non-collapsed) information about the event. Such a theory could also account for the fact that the real-life event is not always a faithful reproduction of the dream. This is a good thing, as many dreams appear to have a warning feature attached to them. If the dreamer changes his behaviour upon realizing that an unpleasant event could possibly unfold in his or her life, the waking ending can be changed somewhat from the dream scenario. Last minute changes reportedly can avert or reduce the impact of these events and examples can be found in

Ryback & Sweitzer. In other words, conscious, focussed intention followed by appropriate behaviour can change the probabilities to produce a more favourable outcome for the dreamer. On the other hand, ignoring or misinterpreting dream material can result in less desirable outcomes. One example is the surgeon that repeatedly dreamed of a brain tumour in his own brain but did not consider that the dreams might actually be portraying his own health condition. As mentioned previously, he died of a brain tumour that might have been treatable at an earlier, less serious stage.

4) The fact that dreamers can dream about the conditions of other people suggests that the brain somehow accesses probable information about others in the same way that it can access information about its own probable future. It is tempting to suggest that the quantum phenomenon of non-locality (entanglement) may somehow be at play here. A substantial number of Heads-Up dreams appear to be about other people. They are often quite accurate and can occur with no respect for distance between dreamer and target. This activity, in a general way, is not unlike the "action at a distance" that entangled particles exhibit. While it might be questioned as to how two unrelated individuals could possibly be entangled, such a theory has been proposed.

If anyone is in doubt that they might at least be genetically related to other human beings, they need only look at the *National Geographic*-sponsored DNA Ancestry project. This is a project that analyzes the DNA of individuals to trace their ancestry back to the beginning of man's life on earth about 175,000 years ago. One of the most interesting findings is that a single female (African) had genes that managed to survive up to modern day while all the rest did not. Thus, we all carry some of those original DNA fragments to this day. It is a small next step to suggest that we are all "entangled," genetically at least.

The above hypotheses are quite speculative, but the ideas provide a beginning. Quantum based principles do provide tempting explanations for phenomena that are considered impossible within the classical physics framework.

⚡ 15 ⚡

Quantum Theory Implications
for Dreaming

To summarize—the idea that there might be a number of possible alternative future life events for each of us does not seem impossible. However, some outcomes are probably more likely than others. People who fly in airplanes have a higher probability of being in an air disaster than those who never fly and insurance companies have made great fortunes working these odds. What is difficult to explain is the fact that sometimes we can see a reasonably accurate depiction of a future waking event in a dream. What are we looking at? It is tempting to suggest that we are seeing a possible event in superposition that has not yet manifest in reality. It is also possible that we are seeing the most probable of the possible waking events to come, because it is the most salient, the most likely to occur in real-life. How then does the individual "see" events concerning someone else? Presumably they are in some way connected to them or entangled with them. The process of attention would probably play a very important role in such a system.

Can the Dreamer Influence Waking Events?

A substantial number of individuals who experience their Heads-Up dreams become waking events fear that they are somehow at least partly responsible for the outcome. While it would seem unlikely that this is true, the idea that the Heads-Up dream induces something to materialize in the real world is worth examining, since in the quantum world, conscious intention appears to do just that under certain conditions.

One of the properties of quantum mechanics is described by Observational Theory. In classical physics, the observer is assumed to be independent and separate from the events that he or she is observing. The idea that you could change an outcome just by watching it happen sounds silly. However, in quantum physics, the observer is not considered to be separate from the object being observed and is believed to actually influence the outcome of experiments. In other words, somehow the mind can influence reality and the act of observing a quantum event influences its outcome.

If we imagine that something like this were possible with the Heads-Up dream—a dream that apparently defies time, we might better explain how something dreamed on a particular night is seen to be a real-life event the following day or next week. If the dreamer is simply observing a probable reality still in superposition, then the apparent time reversal can now be more easily explained. However, a question arises concerning the dreamer. Does the dream observer in some way *influence* the outcome or make it more likely? This would be important in the case of dreaming about a disastrous event like 9/11. As mentioned, dreamers who have Heads-Up dreams sometimes worry that in fact they may have caused an unpleasant real-life event in some way. There is not much evidence to support or refute this idea at the moment, but we can get some hints from the experiences of lucid dreamers.

Lucid Dreaming

Lucid dreamers consider themselves to be consciously aware that they are dreaming. There is a great deal of variability among lucid dreamers, with some simply being aware that they are dreaming while others are able to interact with dream characters and manipulate dream surroundings. Lucid dreaming has not always been accepted as a legitimate experience. However, mainstream science has provided support for this phenomenon and we now have EEG and brain imaging studies to support the description of an activity that lucid dreamers have been telling us about for years.

The original difficulty was to demonstrate that the dreamer could be aware that he or she was dreaming and signal to an awake individual while in rapid eye movement (REM) sleep. Unfortunately, there is almost complete loss of muscle tension during REM sleep— except for the eyes. The problem was solved by having lucid dreamers, with EEG (brain wave) and EOG (eye movement) electrodes on, intentionally send a unique, prearranged signal with their eyes while dreaming. There is now additional evidence from a quantitative EEG experiment that lucid dreamers are conscious during the dream state. Lucid dreamers were observed to show intermediate levels of arousal between non-lucid dreamers in REM sleep and awake individuals. In a brain imaging study, it has been demonstrated that lucid dream activity activates the same brain cells as would the identical waking activity. Lucid dreamers were asked to perform a specific motor task while in the dream. The areas of the brain that were observed to be most active during sleep were the same areas that were observed to be active in the waking individual. Thus, we can be reasonably confident that conscious awareness is possible during REM sleep dreaming. As well, motor activity in dreams appears to utilize the same neurons as does waking motor activity.

Lucid Dreamers and Heads-Up Dreams

Lucid dreamers report a lot of Heads-Up dreams. There is also some anecdotal evidence from lucid dreamers that sometimes, intention plays a part in subsequent waking events. An excellent discussion of these phenomena has been written by Waggoner. Heads-Up dreaming is possible in regular dreams as well as lucid ones. However, the lucid dreamer may be able to add a dimension to this phenomenon regarding the observer problem. How much (if at all) does having a Heads-Up dream add to the probability that the dream scenario will show up in the waking world? Waggoner, based on his own experiences and some of his acquaintances, suggests that there are two kinds of precognitive lucid dreams. The first he labels as "Ambient." In this type of dream, the information that will eventually be a real-life event just seems to be present. It is not requested and not expected, it just seems to be available. For example, Waggoner dreamed

...that he was being chased by gangsters in a car in his old hometown. He drove to hide behind a gas station on a particular street and became lucid when he realized that the gas station was no more. It was now a car wash.

Later in waking life, he found that indeed, the gas station had been torn down and replaced by a carwash in the years since he had left. This was information that he had no previous special interest in and had he not had the dream, might never have noticed the change.

By contrast, it is possible to plan to acquire information about a topic or problem and this kind of lucid dream he has labeled "Active." The conscious intent to find the answer to a specific question about a future event was also explored by Waggoner. When properly planned during waking, he was able to provide himself with the proper dream conditions to get an answer to the question. In one case, he was able to discover a rare genetic condition in the family of a friend. In another instance, he was able to correctly dream the city another friend would be living in one year after the dream. The friend was in a serious relationship at the time of the dream and it seemed as if marriage was imminent. However, the dream also indicated that in his new home, he would be living alone. True to the dream scenario, despite the serious relationship his friend was apparently in at the time, he did not marry the woman and remained single when he moved. The difference between these two types of precognitive dreams may not mean two different dream mechanisms, although the intention to discover a future event could provide a valuable paradigm for studying Heads-Up dream properties.

Can Lucid Dream Intentions Change Waking Outcomes?

In answer to the question of whether the dreams influence real-life outcomes, there are several lucid dream reports that suggest that it depends upon the degree of intention expressed by the dreamer. While simply noting information (ambient) from the dream was quite accurate in predicting a future waking event, it would seem that the actual contribution to the waking outcome by the dreamer was minimal. On the other hand, when the dreamer consciously intended to change something in the lucid dream scenario, it appeared in the subsequent waking event. Most intriguing were some of the health dreams reported. Lucid dreamers were apparently able to change the state of their health for the better in a very short period of time. Ed Kellogg, a very experienced lucid dreamer, reported injuring himself, the result being a dislocated toe with the skin split as well. He received 4 stitches from the doctor, but relocated the toe himself. However, three months later, the foot still bothered him and an aching joint and frequent twinges of pain persisted. He decided, during a lucid dream, to try to heal his toe. This involved "dream chanting"—a healing chant while massaging his toe. Upon awakening, he assessed his toe as 99% better. However, he had a second lucid dream some days later which was more spectacular, in that blue and gold sparks emanated from his hand and were absorbed by his toe. Following this second lucid dream, which he found psychologically more satisfying, he assessed the toe as 100% better and the pains never returned. However, a scar was left from the event and in a third lucid dream, a "yellow laser beam" shot from his fingers to heal it. Following this dream, the scar was virtually gone within a week.

Waggoner describes the case of a woman who was barely able to walk because of six plantar warts on her feet. During the night, she had a lucid dream in which she decided to heal her feet by using a ball of white light (a mental maneuver which she had rehearsed before going to sleep). During the dream, she put her hands on her feet, and the glowing light seemed to enter them. She realized, with great emotion, that she had done what she had planned to do before bed and this woke her up. Her warts had surprisingly all changed from brown to black in colour overnight. Further, all of these warts fell off within ten days. Interestingly, she had tried waking visualizations on her problem feet for some months prior to this experience with no success.

Waggoner has described the health changes in a number of individuals that attempted to "fix" themselves during lucid dreams. Many reported successes, although some did not. He also included a few reports of lucid dreamers being able to positively change the health condition of others.

In trying to decide what factors resulted in lucid dreamers most likely succeeding with their healing attempts, he suggested that attitudes were important. A positive expectation, use of healing techniques that the dreamers could use themselves (however unusual), acceptance of the information provided in the dream, and a willingness to call on inner energy were all valuable factors.

Examination of lucid dream reports of failed attempts to change physical conditions suggested that the dreamer had, at best, a neutral belief or maybe even a negative expectation that change could occur. The dreamers

seemed less willing to accept information and sugges-
tions from the dream, possibly because it conflicted with
waking attitudes and beliefs. The dreamers also seemed
to search for other dream individuals and characters
to do the healing for them, rather than trying to do it
themselves.

Creating Future Events in Others

One report involves an informal experiment by a lucid
dreamer, Ian Wilson, who claims, from time to time, to
have Heads-Up dreams while lucid. One night while
lucid dreaming, he found himself in a familiar environment with a colleague. His male friend was standing
behind a concession counter at work. Feeling that this
might be a Heads-Up type dream and being lucid as well,
he decided to "make" a triangular mark on his friend's
forehead in the dream. He did this by simply pointing at
his friend's head from a distance of about 6 feet and imag-
ining the mark. This design immediately appeared on his
friend's head in the dream. He was not able to verify if
the dream was of the Heads-Up type until about three
weeks later, when, at one point during the day, he realized
that he was experiencing the dream event unfold in real-
life. He found himself in the same environment that he
had been in during the lucid dream. As in the dream, he
pointed his finger at his friend's head behind the concession counter and the triangle appeared as had occurred in
the dream. His friend suddenly had a rather unattractive
red triangular mark on his forehead. There are pictures
of this manifestation that actually rather upset his friend
and persisted for quite sometime. In fact, the dreamer
was not only able to view the probable real-life event,
he was able to change and modify it from his own dream

that occurred 3 weeks before the real-life event. While the lucid dreamer may not have precipitated the general situation in the commercial environment, it could be argued that he did indeed influence the unique blemish on his friend's forehead. He repeated this effect on his own hands. One of the techniques lucid dreamers use to induce lucidity is to examine their hands. This reminds them to ask themselves the question of whether they are dreaming or not, and alerts them to the fact that they are indeed dreaming. Wilson was able to induce a triangle on his own hand in the same way that he had done it to his friend. While this report may seem a little like science fiction, he has gone to a great deal of trouble to verify these events with signed affidavits by witnesses as well as photographs of his own hand and the head of his friend.

The most important thing about this report is that it offers an experimental paradigm that can be used to try to replicate this phenomenon. The idea that one can alter the future is a tantalizing one and suggests that great benefits for the dreamer and others are possible.

Do Heads-Up Dreams Help Induce Reality?

To answer the original question of whether simply dreaming about an event makes it more probable in the real world, there is, as yet, no definitive answer. However, it would seem that there is a great deal of variability in how much the dream activity actually can modulate waking events. At the moment, it seems most likely that simply dreaming of an event which later becomes a waking event, does not measureably change the nature of the waking occurrence. The event would likely have happened anyway. Can we blame a dreamer for the 9/11 disaster in New York simply because he or she reported a dream of seeing the towers in flames and falling down?

And yet, from the lucid dream reports, there would appear to be some dreams that result in some very important physiological changes in subsequent waking events. The degree to which this occurs varies, but there may be gradations of ability to modulate changes in some things. Incidental or ambient information "observed" in the dream would not seem to be made more likely just because it was seen in the dream. However, we have at least anecdotal evidence that intention during lucid dreams is effective in changing or at least modulating the rate at which health improves, both in the dreamer's own body and in the bodies of others. There is virtually no evidence that lucid dream intentions are capable of stopping large world events such as earthquakes or other natural disasters. However, lucid dreaming does provide an interesting opportunity to examine the degree to which future real-life events can be modified or changed during the dream. This is an exciting possibility that could be pursued using standard experimental protocols.

≈ 16 ≈

Do We Really Have Free Will?

The philosophical debate over free will vs. deter-
minism has been going on for many years and will
likely continue for many more. Is there any experimental evidence that free will does or does not exist? At first
glance, Heads-Up dreams suggest that our futures are
pretty much decided for us—at least the segment portrayed by the Heads-Up dream. Interestingly, there are
experimental findings in neuroscience that also suggest
free will is an illusion. In early experiments (over the last
forty years), Libet connected subjects to an EEG brain
wave recording apparatus. The participant was asked to
make simple decisions about events on a screen by press-
ing a button. The brain region involved with this simple
motor activity was observed to be active before the experimental subject consciously "decided" to push the button.
The fact that the brain was already in action before the
choice was consciously made, suggested that consciously
making the decision was an illusion. The appropriate
motor act was already in the process of completing itself.
Since the time between the start of the motor activity
in the brain and the "decision" was only about 0.5 seconds, the results were not convincing to many. However,

a more recent study, using brain imaging techniques has refined and extended this effect. Subjects fixated on a screen and watched a stream of letters go by. On each trial, they were asked to press either a left (hand) or right (hand) button (their free choice) to stop the stream of letters and to remember the letter at which they stopped. On successive trials, subjects were found to have pressed the right and left buttons an equal number of times and were conscious of the decision to press a button 1 second before they actually did it. However, the fMRI brain scan revealed changes in the brain activity of the subjects that preceded the conscious decision of the individual to press a button. The primary motor area (involved in relaying the order to muscles) and frontal-polar cortex (involved in decision making) were observed to become active a whopping seven seconds before the subject "decided" which button to push. Thus, the experimenter knew which decision would be made before the subject him/herself. These results have been interpreted as evidence that free will is an illusion. While we might imagine that we are consciously making our own decisions, they apparently have already been decided at some other level.

These are controversial studies and the conclusion that free will is only an illusion is disappointing for many, myself included. However, the Heads-Up dream may provide some hope for those that like the idea of free will. At the most extreme, it could be argued that because Heads-Up dreams precede waking events, they are destined to occur whether we want them to or not. On the other hand, there are properties about Heads-Up dreams that suggest waking outcomes are not always identical to the dream scenarios.

Do Heads-Up Dreams Mean that the Future is Inevitable?

The extreme possibilities concerning how flexible and different waking events can be, compared to Heads-Up dream scenarios are 1) that the dream represents a preorganized, predestined exact description of what will later manifest in the real world, or 2) the dream is a very flexible probability that an event will occur and if we knew how, we could change one probable outcome for another to avoid unpleasant events and experience more pleasant outcomes.

Considering the first possibility, when one dreams about a scenario that later manifests in the real world, he or she is seeing an event that is apparently already "solidified" at a certain level and not subject to any modification. The subsequent waking event will be a faithful and exact replica of the Heads-Up scenario. This is the view of Gary Schwartz, who has performed one of the more carefully done formal experiments concerning precognitive dreams. The Heads-Up dreamer (Christopher Robin) was able, in advance, to dream the daily events that subsequently took place after the Heads-Up dream scenario had been submitted. His performance led Schwartz to the conclusion that the real-life events in the universe are basically preorganized or predestined in some way, and that some dreamers can see this plan. The Heads-Up dreamer in this case was very good, and certainly his main dream themes were extremely accurate. However, it would be interesting to know if there were at least tiny discrepancies between Robinson's dreams and subsequent waking events. If the idea of a rigid blueprint for the future is true, then any Heads-Up—waking discrepancies would be explained as errors in memory of the dream itself, its interpretation or the limited ability of the dreamer.

At the other end of the spectrum, it could be argued from the Heads-Up dreams I have been examining, that the dream scenario is generally not a completely faithful reproduction of the subsequent waking event, even when there is little or no symbolism. Does this discrepancy indicate that the dream is only a probable description of a future waking event? Is there other evidence to suggest that we are not completely destined to experience waking events according to a prewritten script? While some events are strongly probable and not open to change, others seem more tentative and the possibility of changing the waking outcome exists.

Heads-Up Dream— Waking Event Discrepancies

In the dreams that I have examined, there is little doubt that the waking event is related to the Heads-Up dream, but little details suggest that what is being seen in the dream is not identical to the waking event. It could be argued that this is just because the dream is not remembered correctly. However, because the dreams I have included in this book were all written down in advance of any real-life event, the memory loss theory cannot explain all discrepancies.

Another property of Heads-Up dreams is the presence of symbols. While I have chosen the most literal of Heads-Up dreams for analysis, a few had symbolic references that were clear enough that there was no ambiguity for me. One of the best examples is the dream material of

DM. Her dreams for a patient usually literally portray the exact location or body part involved. On the other hand, if she sees that body part on fire, she has learned that this signifies cancer, and unfortunately for her patients, she has been correct many times.

These dream properties suggest that the Heads-Up dreamer is looking at a scenario that represents a very probable waking event, even if it is not an event that will completely (100%) manifest in the real world in every detail.

Flexibility of Heads-Up Dreams Scenarios

If the Heads-Up dream portrays a giant wave rolling toward a coastal city and the dreamer sees himself or herself drowning, it is unlikely that anything can be done to change the overall waking outcome of flooding, property damage, and loss of life. However, if the time of the disaster was indicated in the dream, then some lives might be saved if anyone heard and believed the dreamer's warning. More realistically, the Heads-Up dreamer might only be able to save him/herself or a close relative or friend. The dream does provide the opportunity for flexibility, but modification of the subsequent waking event is mostly about increasing the safety of the dreamer.

This type of catastrophic world dream can be contrasted with much more mundane Heads-Up dreams. For example, my daughters have used Heads-Up dreams as practical guides in their lives since they were very young. One daughter estimates that she has several Heads-Up dreams per month where she modifies the waking outcome to avoid unpleasant experiences. Some of these dreams depict work situations that she would like to avoid completely. However, she finds that while she can modify the dream endings, and reduce the unpleasant part, many elements of the dream still occur. For example, she dreamed

> ...that I am working at my desk, and waiting for the kettle to boil so I can have some tea. My office mate comes over to talk. While I talk to ML, I inadvertently pour some boiling water on my own foot.

Later that day, she had forgotten the dream until she decided to make herself a cup of hot tea. Her office mate wanted to talk and came over to chat. She then realized that she was in the middle of her Heads-Up dream scenario. To avert disaster, she asked the woman to go back to her desk as she had something important to finish. She took a deep breath, faked doing something important, and let several minutes go by. Then, she continued her day by pouring the kettle and there was no spilling. The office mate was a little puzzled but no harm was done physically or socially.

In a second example she dreamed

> ...that I have a poster mounted on a stand and that I place it in a central area of the building. However, after I put the poster in its spot, I see a red haired security guard take the poster away. The next day when we are all at the event, people ask me why there was no poster to advertise it.

The dream was far from her mind when she decided to take the poster (mounted on a stand) advertising her program and put it in an open area near to where the event would be taking place two days later. She was putting the sign out early as she was not going to be in her office on the following day and she feared that if she left it for someone else, they might forget. She had just left the poster and was walking down the hall with a colleague when she saw a large red-haired security guard pass her, going in the opposite direction—towards her poster. At this point, the memory of the dream kicked in. Her first impulse was to ignore the possibility suggested in the dream—that he might actually remove her poster. But then she decided that she should check. She abruptly left her colleague with an excuse about something important to do and turned back to where the poster had been. Sure enough, he had taken it and put it away, as he had been given strict rules about allowing posters to be displayed outside of certain dates. She could not change his mind, so she retrieved the poster from his storage area and made alternate arrangements. Had she not made the conscious effort, on remembering the dream, to go back, the red-haired security guard would have indeed removed the poster and it would have been missing on the day of the event.

Thus while the main theme of the dream did play out in both cases, being aware of these dreams allowed her to modify the waking life outcomes. In the first, she avoided spilling boiling water on her foot. In the second she managed to reverse the final outcome of the dream scenario by salvaging her poster and getting someone to display it on another day.

Ryback collected and examined hundreds of precognitive dream reports. There were many dreams warning of serious and life threatening situations portrayed by dreamers about themselves and about others. Such dream events as possible car accidents or ill health were modified when the dreamer heeded the dream. The accident was avoided and the sick person did not die because of timely attention to the problem. These waking outcomes were much preferable to the dream scenarios. In one case, a woman dreamed that her son would be in an airplane crash. She was not close to her son, but at the urging of a friend, did telephone him. She told him things that she had intended to tell him for some time, but had not gotten around to it. Unfortunately, she did not tell him about her dream, and tragically he did die in a plane crash, just as she had seen. While she could not bring her son back, she was glad that she had had one recent serious personal conversation with him before he died. It was not the best alternate outcome, but better than nothing and we can only wonder what would have happened had she told her son the dream.

Heads-Up Health Dreams

Some of the most important Heads-Up dreams seem to involve the health of the individual. They can portray nasty health problems (such as my smoking dream) that seem to make them obvious warning dreams. The dream is describing a situation that is apparently serious—but not yet fatal.

In some cases it is possible to follow the progression and intensity of a series of dreams concerning a single health problem. In the dreams of DM concerning her mother, it was possible to follow the progression of real-life events, the warning dreams and the consequences of not heeding these dreams. Because DM had so many dreams about her mother's health, it is possible to get a more comprehensive look at how the dream scenarios are related to the waking events. For example, in early dreams about her mother, DM dreamed that she was at health risk because she was using a particular kind of medication. In fact, she dreamed about this medication before her mother admitted that she was using it. The initial dreams were about a particular book and she was able to eventually discover in subsequent dreams that a steroid mentioned in the book, was not a suitable medication, as it was cancer inducing. We can only speculate what would have happened if her mother had simply stopped the steroid medication after those dreams, but one might expect that DM's dreams about her mother's health would have ceased. There might not have been such an unpleasant future for her and she might have enjoyed better health. However, since she did not heed the warnings, the dreams clearly became more negative and provided more unpleasant scenarios. Dreams about surgery and prolonged medication began to occur. In one of the last dreams before her mother went to the hospital, there appeared to be a fire in a building, an urgent dream warning of serious waking events. The progression of these Heads-Up dreams seems to be in step with the increasing severity of the illness (and way out of step with the doctor). By the time DM had the dream about a fire in the building, it was too late to reconsider stopping the steroid medication. The cancer had progressed dangerously and the probability of a positive outcome diminished.

While we are a long way from deciding how much flexibility is possible following Heads-Up dream occurrences, there is apparently some "wiggle room" to modify the intensity of involvement in the dream scenario, especially with regard to the dreamer him/herself. Intentional changes seem to modify the waking outcome of the event compared to the dream, although a substantial part of the Heads-Up dream scenario still plays out. For even the starkest of Heads-Up dreams, the role of the dreamer can be modified, although the main part of the scenario still occurs. In the case of someone dreaming about the waking outcome of someone else, the same applies. The value of these Heads-Up dreams—other than to provide a picture of a very probable future, may be to allow for this flexibility. Without such flexibility, the usefulness of the Heads-Up dream seems quite limited and could, in the case of negative Heads-Up dreams serve only to raise the dreamer's stress level—not a very helpful survival mechanism. If Heads-Up dream scenarios are really cast in stone, then it might actually be better not to remember dreams at all and to be "blind-sided" by the events of each day so that pre-disaster ignorance would be bliss.

Is the Heads-Up Dream a Superposition State?

At the moment, it would seem that merely dreaming about an event that manifests in the future does not enhance its probability of occurrence. To use a quantum mechanical metaphor, the event "observed" by the ordinary dreamer does not make it "collapse" into reality. The Heads-Up dream is apparently a probable event already in a fairly robust form. On the other hand, it is not yet an event in the waking world. My best guess at this point is that the Heads-Up dream represents some kind of quasi-permanent event that is not yet "real," but is more probable than it was and it is urgent that the dreamer take "waking" action now. Adding conscious intention, during dream lucidity, apparently can modify the waking outcome to some extent. However, now the dreamer is not just passively looking at the dream scenario, but is exerting some kind of influence during the dream itself.

Tampering with the future may not have consequences as serious as the "butterfly effect" (originated by Edward Lorenz and based in chaos theory). According to this idea, if one could travel back in time and tamper with anything at all, even accidently killing a butterfly in this earlier time—the result would be a radically different "now" world. We may not be travelling back in time in Heads-Up dreams, rather we may be seeing the partial "solidification" of eventual waking events at some level. There is still some leeway in the outcome, especially for the dreamer, but the time for remedial real world action is limited.

⇒ 17 ⇐

Capturing Dreams

If you are someone who remembers at least one dream per night and often two or three dreams, then you should probably skip the next section. On the other hand, if you seldom remember your dreams and have problems remembering them, read on. I have never found remembering my dreams an easy task and have to work on it constantly, to this day. Dreams come at regular intervals in the night (there is a REM sleep period every 90 minutes). When you do have a dream in the middle of the night, you are often aware of this, but tell yourself that you will write it down in the morning. (You likely won't. Kiss those dreams good-bye.) If I have a dream in the middle of the night, I try to record the main details immediately. There are a number of methods one can use and I have tried them all. The tape recorder is one possibility. It works for some, but I am quite incoherent at 3 AM and often don't understand what I said when I replay the episode. Further, you do risk waking your partner or other family members. I have settled on the technique of writing down the basic theme of the dream on a page fastened to a clipboard. At first I used a flashlight, but this not only aroused my wife, but I awakened to the extent that I was then often unable to recall the dream. The use of a special pen-light device was better, but turned out not to be my favourite. My preferred method is to write down the theme in pencil in the dark. As it turns out, it is possible to form the letters without a light and understand the writing well enough that in the morning, reading the scrawl is enough to bring back the entire dream. I make sure I have a clipboard with fresh paper and a pencil attached.

Trying to remember a dream in the morning, as you wake up, can also be difficult. In order to maximize chances, I recommend that as you wake up, there be complete silence. The sound of an alarm usually is sufficient to erase all but my most salient dreams. Thus, if you wake up to a clock radio or loud obnoxious alarm, your chances of remembering the dream may be minimal, although, to my amazement, this is not a problem for some. If you talk to your partner, a child or have to deal with a pet—again—your chances of remembering the dream are reduced. I have often resorted to lying exactly as I awoke and remember that I have a task—I want to remember my dream. I run it through my mind several times in order to memorize it well enough that I can delay writing it down until after I have done some of the regular morning rituals such as shaving, showering, talking to children, etc. Often all of these things have intervened before I get to my computer. In fact, middle-of-the-night dreams with only my scrawl made in the dark are sometimes the only ones preserved.

If you have trouble waking up enough in the night to bother writing down your dream, drink a large glass of water before bed. This will ensure that you wake up in order to make a trip to the bathroom but—be sure to write

Head's-Up Dreaming

the dream before starting your journey to the bathroom or you will likely lose it. Waking or a lightening of sleep usually happens just at the end of a REM period at the completion of a dream. If you cannot wake up enough, you can always resort to the artificial timed awakening. Since your REM dreams come at regular 90 minute intervals during the night, estimate your sleep onset time and then set the alarm for 3 hours, 4h 30 minutes or 6 hours later. (The first REM period dream, completed about 90 minutes after sleep onset is usually quite short and is especially hard to remember. Skip it.)

Recording Your Own Heads-Up Dreams

1) Recording of the dream must be done first thing upon awakening. The dreamer must plan to try to do this as often as possible. I can muster 4–5 dreams a week at best, although some individuals remember at least one dream every night. *Once the dream is written down, it cannot be changed in the dreamer's mind to fit any real-life event that occurs later the same day or in the next days or weeks. It can then be carefully compared to any life event that seems connected to the dream later on. As is usually the case there will be a number of remarkable hits, but also some details that are not exact, even though, overall, the dream will have Heads-Up properties.*

2) Writing down your dreams each morning, can seem a bit time consuming, but once you actually discover a Heads-Up dream, you will be more motivated. *Some 10–15% of your dreams will likely be of the Heads-Up type, so you may need to collect 20–30 of them before you begin to notice any of the Heads-Up type.*

3) In writing down the dream, I have found the following details are important. Start by putting down the date. *I note whether the dream is early in the night, the middle of the night or the last one I had before waking up in the morning. This may not be absolutely necessary, but it may help you to notice patterns in your dreaming.*

4) Give the dream a title that describes its content as much as possible. *Then on computer, you can scroll through older dreams and get an idea about the content without having to open the file. In reviewing dreams, it is possible just to look at the title and note if a dream might have anything to do with a day event. It is much faster than re-reading whole dreams.*

5) The dream itself should be recorded separately from any thoughts or comments that you might have about it. *It is important not to begin judging the meaning or importance of the dream material when recording it. The conscious mind is only too willing to begin to edit the material immediately.* I have, on some occasions found myself deciding that the dream material isn't all that important anyway. Amazingly, some dream material that I managed to preserve despite these urges turned out to be quite remarkable. The decision making part of the brain is not functioning very well at this point and should be ignored. For example, I had, on awakening, judged a bizarre dream of flying over Lake Michigan high above the Chicago sky scrapers of the Golden Mile as not being very interesting and not worthy of writing down. This demonstrates how poorly the evaluative function of the brain works prior to complete arousal. Later, when fully awake, the dream can take on a much more amazing quality.

6) Following the dream record, I reserve a section for comments. Again, I date the comments made and have often returned even years later to add more comments about a particular dream. It is here that you can discuss any noted relationship between the dream and corresponding waking events. You can also record any unusual activities in which you have been participating, any medications you have been taking, etc. *While it is possible to keep your records in books, or worse, on individual pieces of paper in folders, I have long since abandoned these techniques in favour of the computer.*

7) As well, if you can get a partner or friend to tell you their dreams each day and you also write these down, you can double your chances of seeing Heads-Up dreams. *In fact it is sometimes easier to spot them for others than for yourself. All of this is time consuming and while I still keep a day diary, I have given up writing down most of my wife's dreams on a regular basis and my children are now grown and live in other cities. While certainly optional, keeping a day diary of events is also helpful.*

8) If you feel the need to draw something you "saw," try to scan and merge the drawing with the text of the dream, so the two are together. *One of the drawbacks of using a computer is the disconnect between the text and a drawing of something seen in the dream that simply cannot be verbally described. When I kept my dreams on individual pieces of paper, and lost or misplaced some, it was at least easy to add a sketch, with colour if required, to the dream. The process is more complicated and time consuming with a computer, but can be done. Sometimes the drawing seems essential.*

Recognizing the Heads-Up Dream

1) *Recognition of Heads-Up dreams is always made easier when they involve the unusual and unexpected in your life.* People that you have not seen for years, unusual places that you go to that were not previously planned, presence of distinctive objects—all of these things help you to realize that the dream has indeed preceded the life event that has occurred.

2) *The discovery of a Heads-Up will usually happen when something in your waking day reminds you of the dream. If several dream elements are similar to the real-life event, then you may have a Heads-Up dream.* I like to see at least two and hopefully three "hits" or correspondences between the dream events and the subsequent waking events.

3) *There is a little twinge of recognition that often happens when you make a dream/real-life connection.* It may just be a cognitive feeling of recognition, but there may also be some kind of physiological reaction such as a shiver or "goose bumps." As described so well by Dunne, at first you will only notice one dream element that is connected to the real-life event. Then as you reflect on the situation, you realize that there are several correspondences. At some point there will be a sort of inner feeling of discovery that you may have had a Heads-Up experience.

4) *The easiest Heads-Ups to spot are of the "same day" type and these will likely be noticed first. But the delayed dreams can be quite important.* Dreams that appear to be complete nonsense on the day they are written and for several days after, can sometimes suddenly seem a lot like real-life events weeks later.

5) *If at all possible, share your dreams with someone that will take an interest in your project. This will increase the probability of seeing a Heads-Up dream.* Often, as mentioned before, the dreamer is not that good at noticing dream/waking connections. The "blind spot" is a very potent phenomenon. Conversely, if you collect or listen to the dreams of another, you might spot a Heads-Up type dream that they simply did not notice.

6) *Typically, the Heads-Up dream is a relatively short dream that occurs just as you are waking up. Short and long are relative and you must judge for yourself what this means to your individual dream reports. Long, emotional dreams are probably not Heads-Up dreams and many of your dreams will not be of the Heads-Up type.* To clarify, this does not mean you should ignore middle of the night or long dreams. The important point is that often, the Heads-Up part of the dream sometimes seems to be tacked on to the end of a longer, rambling dream and may even seem a little different in content. This is not a hard and fast rule, but it often happens to me and has also been noted by my Heads-Up dream colleagues.

7) *There is not likely to be many scene shifts in your Heads-Up dream.* A quick count of number of scene shifts or changes in dream settings will help you to assess the probability of your dream being of the Heads-Up type. Lots of scene shifts suggest that the dream may not be a Heads-Up.

8) *The Heads-Up dream is typically not emotional at the time, more a statement of fact.* It may be about emotionally upsetting things, but tends to be delivered in a neutral tone.

9) *Read your old dreams over once a week or so.* Often a dream just written makes no sense whatsoever. However, the same dream a week or so later can be quite revealing and you may notice correspondences between dream events and something currently going on in your life.

Heads-Ups tend to be more literal, possibly due to the fact that they are time-sensitive and require immediate action.

Incubating Dreams

1) If you *want* to have a dream about a specific problem of your own, you will need to be patient. This is the hardest thing to do, as it usually involves trying to get information about someone or something very important to you. Because of the emotion involved, you may not allow yourself to have this dream easily and will have to persist for several nights. Some alternatives include writing the question down and putting it under your pillow. Or sitting for 10 minutes or so repeating the question to yourself before bed. Remember—part of you wants to know, but possibly part of you does not want to know or is frightened of the whole thing, so it can take several nights.

2) The dream may not make any sense at first. Nevertheless, as time goes on, you may realize that it does, especially as your life unfolds.

3) Dreaming for someone else is a bit exhausting, but you may get more immediate results. When you are trying to help someone else, you will be more likely to write the dream down because of the obligation you feel to help them.

4) Don't try to second-guess or evaluate the importance of the dream material at the time you have it. Your logical decision making frontal cortex is not working. Dreams considered to be nonsense on waking may look much more relevant and valuable the next day or next week.

Working with Your Heads-Ups Dreams

It is important to understand your own dream language in order to encode symbolism in dreams. (e.g. fire in a body part could represent cancer. These symbols tend to recur.) There is no shortcut here. While the dream symbol might happen to be the same as that of someone else or a dream book symbol item—it might just be unique and you will only learn what it signifies by seeing it go by a number of times.

You may spontaneously or intentionally have a dream about someone else. If that dream seems important or urgent (possibly having to do with health or safety) there are some guidelines you should follow:

1) It is important for you, the dreamer, to communicate with the dreamed individual in order to confirm that you're on the right track. Contact the individual, no matter how silly it might seem.

2) You will find that there is usually an opportunity to bring up the dream during the conversation and most of the time it "hits a nerve."

3) Surprisingly, the dreamed information is rarely a shock to the person and they usually respond by noting a connection between the dream and their own real-life activity.

4) Often there is a connection between your dream and their real-life situation.

5) To shy away from contacting the dreamed individual could result in a missed opportunity to help someone.

6) Editing or ignoring parts of the dream that don't seem relevant usually results in discarding valuable information.

7) The ability to have these dreams is not restricted to a few special individuals. Almost anyone can experience this phenomenon if they are alert to the possibility.

The rules and guidelines I have presented above are not necessarily exhaustive and you may be able to add to them, but they will get you started Heads-Up dreaming. After forty years of Heads-Up dreaming, I can safely say that it will certainly enrich your life and give you some added information about the many difficult major decisions you must make despite not having complete waking information and despite the strong opinions of others. Heads-Up dreams can provide your very best advice.

Chapter Notes

Chapter 1

Aserinsky, E., and Kleitman, N. (1953). Regularly occurring periods of eye motility, and concomitant phenomena, during sleep. *Science* 118:273-274.

Funkhouser, A.T. (1983a). The dream theory of déjà vu. *Parapsychological Journal of South Africa* 4:107-123.

_____ (1983b). A historical review of déjà vu. *Parapsychological Journal of South Africa* 4:11-24.

Funkhouser, A.T., and Schredl, M. (2010). The frequency of déjà vu (déjà rêvé) and the effects of age, dream recall frequency and personality factors. *International Journal of Dream Research* 3:60-64.

Chapter 3

Funkhouser, A.T., and Schredl, M. (2010). The frequency of déjà vu (déjà rêvé) and the effects of age, dream recall frequency and personality factors. *International Journal of Dream Research* 3:60-64.

Chapter 4

Rhine, L.E. 1961. *Hidden Channels of the Mind.* William Sloan Associates, New York.

Van de Castle, R.L., Dwyer, R.V. and Pimm, B.A. 2010. Dreams as a multidimensional expression of psi. *Explore* 6:263-268.

Chapter 7

Domhoff, G.W. 2003. The scientific study of dreams: neural networks, cognitive development and content analysis. American Psychological Association, Washington.

_____ 2010. Dream content is continuous with waking thought, based on preoccupations, concerns, and interests *Sleep Medicine Clinics* 5:203-215.

Hall, C., and Van de Castle, R.L. 1966. *The Content Analysis of Dreams*. Appleton-Century-Crofts, New York.

Van de Castle, R.L. 1994. *Our Dreaming Mind*. Ballentine, New York.

Chapter 8

Dunne, J.W. 1927. *An Experiment with Time*. A & C Black Ltd., London.

Schwartz, G.E. 2006. *The G.O.D. Experiments*. Atria Books, New York.

_____ 2011. Exploratory blinded field experiment evaluating purported precognitive dreams in a highly skilled subject: possible spiritual mediation? *The Journal of Spirituality and Paranormal Studies* 34:3-20.

Ullman, M., Krippner, S. and Vaughn, A. 1989. *Dream Telepathy: Experiments in Nocturnal ESP*. McFarland & Company, Jefferson, NC.

Van de Castle, R.L. 1994. *Our Dreaming Mind*. Ballentine, New York.

Chapter 9

Garfield, P. 1991. *The Healing Power of Dreams*. Simon & Shuster, New York.

Leuthold, A. 2008. Illness as foretold in dreams. Paper presented at the International Association for the Study of Dreams, June 6-12, Montreal.

Smith, R. 1986. Evaluating dream function: Emphasizing the study of patients with organic disease. In Cognition and Dream Research. R. Haskell (Ed.), Institute of Mind and Behavior, Orono, Maine.

Van de Castle, R.L. 1994. *Our Dreaming Mind*. Ballentine, New York.

Chapter 11

Reed, H. (2005). The dream helper ceremony: The "good smaritan" dreaming circle in *Dream Medicine: Learning How To Get Help From Our Dreams*. In H. Reed (Ed.), We Publish Books, Rancho Mirage , CA.

Ullman, M., S. Krippner, and A. Vaughn. (1989). *Dream Telepathy: Experiments in Nocturnal ESP*. McFarland & Company, Jefferson, NC.

Van de Castle, R.L., Dwyer, R.V. and Pimm, B.A. (2010). Dreams as a multidimensional expression of psi. *Explore* 6:263-268.

Chapter 12

Hall, C., and Van de Castle, R.L.. 1966. *The Content Analysis of Dreams*. Appleton-Century-Crofts, New York.

Smith, C.T. 2013. Can healthy, young adults uncover personal details of unknown target individuals in their dreams? *Explore* 9:17-25.

Chapter 13

Bird, W.R. (2002). *Ghosts have warm hands*. CEF Books, Ottawa.

Broughton, R.S. (1988). *If You Want to Know How it Works, First Find Out What it is For*. In, Research in Parapsychology 1987. D.H. Weiner, and R.L. Morris (Eds). The Scarecrow Press, 187-202.

_____ (2006). Memory, emotion and the receptive process. *The Journal of Parapsychology* 70:255-274.

Radin, D.I. (2006). *Entangled Minds*. Pocket Books, New York.

Ryback, D. and Sweitzer, L. (1988). *Dreams that Come True*. Ballantine, New York.

Smith, C.T. (2010). Sleep states, memory processing and dreams. *Sleep Medicine Clinics* 5:217-228.

Waggoner, R. (2009). *Lucid Dreaming: Gateway to the Inner Self*. Moment Point Press, Needham, MA.

Chapter 14

Al-Khalili, J. (2003). *Quantum: A Guide for the Perplexed*. Weidenfeld & Nicolson, London.

Bem, D.J. (2011). Feeling the future: Experimental evidence for anomalous retroactive influences on cognition and affect. *Journal of Personality and Social Psychology* 100:407-425.

Bierman, D.J. (1998). *Do Psi Phenomena Suggest Radical Dualism?* In *Toward a Science of Consciousness II*. S. Hameroff, A.W. Kaszniac, and A.C. Scott (Eds.) MIT Press, Cambridge, MA. 709-714.

Cai, J., Gracomo, G. and Briegel, H.J. (2010) Quantum control and entanglement in a chemical compass. *Physical Review Letters* 104: 220502-1 - 220502-4.

Collini, E., Wong, C.Y., Wilk, K.E., Curmi, P.M.G., Brumer, P. and Scholes, G.D. (2010). Coherently wired light-harvesting in photosynthetic marine algae at ambient temperature. *Nature* 463:644-647.

Dunne, B.J., and Jahn, R.G.. (2003). Information and uncertainty in remote perception research. *Journal of Scientific Exploration* 17:207-241.

Franco, M.I., Turin, L., Mershin, A., and Skoulakis, E.M.C. (2011). Molecular vibration sensing component in Drosphila Melanogaster olfaction. *Proceedings of the National Academy of Science* 108:3797-3802.

Gauger, E.M., Rieper, E., Morton, J.J.L., Benjamin, S.C. and Vedral, V. (2011). Sustained quantum coherence and entanglement in the avian compass. *Physical Review Letters* 106: 040503-1 - 040503-4.

Goswami, A. 1993. *The Self-Aware Universe*. Tarcher/Putnam, New York.

Hameroff, S., and Penrose, R. (1996). Conscious events as orchestrated space-time selections. *Journal of Consciousness Studies* 3:36-53.

Kaftos, M., and Nadeau, R. (1999). *The Conscious Universe: Parts and Wholes in Physical Reality*. Oxford University Press, New York.

Leuthold, A. (2008). Illness as Foretold in Dreams. Paper presented at the International Association for the Study of Dreams, June 6-12, Montreal.

Pribram, K.H. (1991). *Brain and Perception: Holonomy and Structure in Figural Processing*. Lawrence Earlbaum Associates, Hillsdale, N.J.

Radin, D.I. (2006). *Entangled Minds*. Pocket Books, New York.

Rauscher, E., and Targ, R. (2001). The Speed of Thought: The investigation of a complex space-time metric to describe psychic phenomena. *Journal of Scientific Exploration* 15:331-354.

_____ (2006). Investigation of a complex space-time metric to describe precognition of the future. In *Frontiers of Time: Retrocausation-Experiment and Theory*, D.P. Sheehan (Ed.) Melville, San Diego, CA.

Rosenblum, B., and Kuttner, F. (2006). *Quantum Enigma: Physics Encounters Consciousness*. Oxford University Press, New York.

Ryback, D., and Sweitzer, L. (1988). *Dreams that Come True*. Ballantine, New York.

Smith, C.T. (2013). Can healthy, young adults uncover personal details of unknown target individuals in their dreams? *Explore* 9:17-25.

Talbot, M.C. (1991). *The Holographic Universe*. Harper Collins, New York.

Walach, H. (2005). Generalized Entanglement: a new theoretical model for understanding the effects of complementary and alternative medicine. *Journal of Alternative and Complementary Medicine* 11:549-559.

Chapter 15

Dresler, M., Koch, S.P., Wehrle, R., Spoormaker, V.I., Holsboer, F. Steiger, A. Samann, P.G., Obrig, H. and Czisch, M. (2011). Dreamed movement elicits activation in the sensorimotor cortex. *Current Biology* 21:1833-1837.

Kellogg III, E.W. (1989). A personal experience in lucid dream healing. *The Lucidity Letter* 8:6-7.

LaBerge, S. (1990). Lucid Dreaming: Psychophysiological studies of consciousness during REM sleep. In Sleep and Cognition. R.R. Bootzen, J.F. Kihlstrom, and D.L. Schacter

(Eds.). American Psychological Association, Washington, D.C. 109-126.

Radin, D.I. (2006). *Entangled Minds*. Pocket Books, New York.

Voss, U., Holzmann, R., Tuin, I. and Hobson, J.A. (2009). Lucid dreaming: a state of consciousness with features of both waking and non-lucid dreaming. *Sleep* 32:1191-1200.

Waggoner, R. (2009). *Lucid Dreaming: Gateway to the Inner Self*. Moment Point Press, Needham, MA.

Walach, H. (2005). Generalized Entanglement: a new theoretical model for understanding the effects of complementary and alternative medicine. *Journal of Alternative and Complementary Medicine* 11:549-559.

Wilson, I. (2011). Déjà Vu or Déjà Rêvé? *http://www .youaredreaming.org/assets/pdf/deja_vu_or_deja_reve.pdf*

Chapter 16

Libet, B. (2004). *Mind Time: the Temporal Factor in Consciousness*. Harvard University Press, Cambridge, Massachusetts.

Libet, B., Wright, E.W.and Gleason, C.A. (1982). Readiness-potentials preceding unrestricted "spontaneous" vs. pre-planned voluntary acts. *Electroencephalograpy & Clinical Neurophysiology* 54:322-335.

Ryback, D., and Sweitzer, L. (1988). *Dreams that Come True*. Ballantine, New York.

Schwartz, G.E. (2011). Exploratory blinded field experiment evaluating purported precognitive dreams in a highly skilled subject: possible spiritual mediation? *The Journal of Spirituality and Paranormal Studies* 34:3-20.

Soon, C.S., Brass, M., Heinze, H.-J. and Haynes, J.D. (2008). Unconscious determinants of free decisions in the human brain. *Nature Neuroscience* 11:543-545.

About the Author

Carlyle Smith, Ph.D., C. Psych. is Lifetime Professor Emeritus of Psychology at Trent University, Peterborough, Ontario, Canada and is Director of Trent University Sleep Research Laboratories. He has published widely on the topics of sleep, memory and dreams and has taught courses on these topics for over 30 years. His work has been the subject of numerous radio and TV documentaries in both North America and Europe. Dr. Smith was awarded the Trent University Distinguished Research Award in 2000 and the Canadian Sleep Society Distinguished Scientist Award in 2009.